P

The Powe

MW00986930

"*The Power of One Man* is written to underscore the truth that God does not call the qualified, but He qualifies whom He calls. Ron's newest book will make it clear that all men were born with a God-given mission, a message to fulfill their divine design.

"This book, like Ron the speaker, is inspiring, motivating, and a perfect manifesto on God's restoration process to redeem men.

"I find Ron humble, supportive, and dedicated. He is a great servant leader who has a heart for broken men. This book will help your husband, brother, son, or nephew to transform their pain into power and their wounds into wisdom. Get this book into the hands of a broken man in your life and watch God show up."
　—STEVE ARTERBURN
　　President of New Life Ministries

"*The Power of One Man* is a must-read. Ron's book is life-changing, full of hope, and confirms the fact that God can use ordinary men to do extraordinary things.

"We believe God has called Ron Archer for such a time as this. His life story testifies to the fact that God can turn 'our test into a testimony; your mess into message, and your trial into triumph.' Ron, you are indeed a sermon in shoes. Keep writing."
　—EDDIE AND MARIONNE TUCKER
　　Founders of His Glory Revealed Ministries

"A few years ago, I had the privilege of attending a meeting with all the congressional representatives of our country, the Dominican Republic. The most important religious leaders were also in attendance.

"The guest speaker gave a keynote speech full of energy, wisdom, and knowledge, capturing the attention of everyone in the room. What struck me the most was the presence of God that he carried. His name was Dr. Ron Archer. This anointed man of God blessed us in such a profound way.

"With *The Power of One Man*, Dr. Archer takes us on a journey exploring manhood in the light of the Scriptures, developing a complete analysis and dealing with the global problem of fatherlessness and all the issues every man faces in a direct, clear, and at the same time very profound manner.

"By reading this book, you will have the experience of receiving not just information, but transformation. Every written word on these pages will touch not only your intellect but your heart."

—APOSTLE RAFAEL CRUZ LORA
    Senior pastor at Iglesia Pentecostal Shekinah in the
    Dominican Republic

"I love this book! The fatherlessness that plagues this country carries so many questions, but few have penned the answer as well as Dr. Archer has in this clear and precise book. It's like a road map for any young or older man that didn't have a father figure in his life. He no longer has to be a victim. He can rise above it and be the dad that he didn't have. As a pregnancy center founder, my heart has been to reach and teach our dads, to give them what they have not had; this book will go into the hands of these dads in our centers. Thank you, Dr. Archer."

—VIKKI PARKER
    Founder and executive director at Options Pregnancy
    Centers

"We live in a world where a lot of men struggle with their identity since there has been no role model or mentor to point out the right direction. Your story sheds light on how God can draw one man from obscurity into notoriety and bring him to a place of stability and impact if he will allow it.

"Your story shows us that your background doesn't matter but your future does. There are no excuses for remaining where you are or blaming it on your past or on others. An attitude and mindset submitted to God will take you to your divine purpose and destiny."

—SIFISO BRIAN MAZIBUKO
Lead pastor at Jesus Calls Worship Centre-Midrand in Johannesburg, South Africa

"*The Power of One Man* is a must-read. One sometimes speaks of helplessness or loneliness, but Ronaldo Archer saw how God has used one man at different points in history to transform what God needed changed.

"Most of the time, the one was small yet had a great job to perform. This book shows how powerful you can be if you can look inside and turn negatives into positives. This book will take you from low to high if you can only imagine it being possible."

—CHERRYL JORDAN JONES
Librarian for the Open Bible Institute of Theology in San Fernando, Trinidad

"Some books educate, some make you think, and a few will inspire you; this book will do all three.

"Reading *The Power of One Man* will change your perspective. It's not meant to make you a 'better' man but to share the greatness God has already created in you and how He longs to use men just like you and me. Dr. Archer shares God's heart toward US and provides hope and encouragement through relevant stories and biblical truths."

—THOM COLLIER
Commissioner in Knox County, Ohio

The Power of One Man

THE POWER OF
ONE MAN

How God Uses Men Like You
to Change the World

RON ARCHER
WITH MIKE YORKEY

SALEM
BOOKS
an imprint of Regnery Publishing
Washington, D.C.

Salem Books™ is a trademark of Salem Communications Holding Corporation
Regnery® is a registered trademark of Salem Communications Holding Corporation

ISBN: 978-1-68451-053-5
eISBN: 978-1-68451-143-3

Library of Congress Control Number: 2020945140

Published in the United States by
Salem Books
An Imprint of Regnery Publishing
A Division of Salem Media Group
Washington, D.C.
www.SalemBooks.com

Manufactured in the United States of America

10 9 8 7 6 5 4 3 2 1

Books are available in quantity for promotional or premium use. For information on discounts and terms, please visit our website: www.SalemBooks.com

To my three grandchildren—
Nehemiah Lance Archer, Noelani Michelle Archer,
and Kaila Moore—and their futures

CONTENTS

PART I

Setting Down Markers

1

How One Man Can Change Everything

Seated in a folding chair, I straightened my red tie as I watched Father O'Connell, the principal of St. Peter Chanel High School, step toward a wooden podium planted at the half-court line of our basketball gymnasium. It was a Friday morning in May. The year was 1980.

"Chanel Men, welcome to this special assembly," began the Roman Catholic priest, dressed in his customary black suit with a white Roman collar. "Last week, you watched our three candidates for next year's student body president participate in a televised debate. Today, we're going to hear from each candidate in person. I urge you to give each one the respect they deserve for this important position."

I was one of the three candidates; all of us were juniors at Chanel High. As I sat in my chair, waiting for my turn, I remembered how Father O'Connell had called me into his office a month earlier.

Normally, a summons to the principal's office meant only one thing: I was in trouble. I racked my brain to think what I'd done, but

I'd been a model student: the starting quarterback on the football team, an active member of the debate club, and the anchor of the student news broadcast at the start of each school day on closed-circuit TV. Teachers liked me. So did my fellow classmates. I thought I got along well with everyone.

Father O'Connell immediately set my mind at ease as he escorted me away from his imposing cherrywood desk toward a loveseat upholstered in burgundy leather.

"Please, sit down," the priest said as he slid into a leather armchair across from me. "I have a proposition for you."

I couldn't imagine what it might be. "What are you thinking, Father?" I asked.

Father O'Connell hitched his black slacks and looked me in the eye.

"I want to make history with you. I would like you to run for student body president," the priest said. "Chanel needs to change. We need to grow, and we need to diversify our school. You're just the man to do that."

You're just the man to do that.

Hearing Father O'Connell say those words filled my sails with billowy gusts of encouragement. It was like he was saying, "Son, come stand with us, shoulder to shoulder. You belong. You're becoming a man."

Then the kindly priest uttered some profound words that have stuck with me all these years. "Sometimes, Ron, a young man can pick his time, but sometimes the time picks the young man," he said. "I believe this is your time, son. You're articulate and well-spoken. You're an athlete, and you're doing well in school. Your classmates respect you. If you run, I firmly believe you can become our next student body president."

I was humbled by his words and thought about how I had tried to show leadership at Chanel, an all-boys Catholic high school with five hundred students that was named after St. Peter Chanel, a nineteenth-century French missionary martyred in 1841 while living among South

Pacific islanders. Leading our football team had to count for something, as well as how I had taken the initiative to hold Bible studies in the school cafeteria during our lunch breaks. But becoming president of the senior class of 1981? There was still a seed of self-doubt within me.

"Are you sure the school is ready for this? We both know Chanel is more than 90 percent white," I commented. It seemed to me that my black skin could be a hurdle for some people.

Father O'Connell rose out of his chair and started pacing around the office. "You know what?" he asked, his voice an octave higher. "I want you to stop thinking that way. People do not see you as a color."

"Really?" This seemed hard to believe.

"Yes. From all my interactions with the students and hearing what they say about you, it's almost like you're translucent."

"What do you mean by that?"

"They see you as Ron Archer, the person—not as someone who's black or white or Hispanic or Cuban. You appeal to everybody. You're a natural-born leader who knows the Bible as well as any priest. That's why I want you to run."

With support like that, I had to throw my hat into the ring.

Right off the bat, my pair of simple homemade posters didn't stack up well against the professionally done signs that my two competitors pasted on their friends' lockers all along the main hallway. Mine displayed a picture of me standing next to my family's Christmas tree with my mom and my sister. My handwritten headline said:

Faith, Family, Future
Vote Ron Archer for Student Body President

Maybe my posters were underwhelming, but I had a secret weapon: my ability to marshal my thoughts, speak in public, and show poise before audiences. After our first debate in front of a TV camera, I felt that addressing my fellow students live and in person inside the gymnasium would change the score to "Advantage Archer."

Father O'Connell looked to the bleachers, right and then left, filled with Chanel students dressed in gray slacks and white button-down shirts. "We'll hear first from John Malloy, who will give us his opening statement, and then from our other candidates. After that, they will tell us why they deserve your vote," the school principal said.

"Hello," John began somewhat awkwardly, pausing for a beat too long as he studied a sheet of paper in his hand. His normally rosy cheeks looked like they were on fire from nerves and embarrassment.

"I'm John Malloy, and I'm running for student body president for Chanel High," he continued. "All I can promise you is that with your vote, we can work together to make our time in high school the best it can possibly be. We will use teamwork to raise money and improve class trips. I will put all my time and effort into making our class the best it can be. If we unite and put a lot of effort into our fundraising activities, we can make a ton of money. The more money we have, the more fun high school will be. So please vote for me."

With that, John stepped aside to a smattering of applause as Father O'Connell returned to the podium to introduce Bill Buchanan.

I knew I would be introduced last, which gave me time to think about how far I'd come since my sophomore year, when I started attending the school, which was located in the middle- and upper-class white neighborhood of Bedford, Ohio. I had to sit on a bus for more than an hour one-way to get to school each morning because I lived twelve miles away in downtown Cleveland—more specifically, a predominantly black neighborhood known as Lee-Harvard.

The fact that I had been accepted for enrollment at Chanel was a minor miracle. I came from the Cleveland public school system, where kids like myself were several grade levels behind when it came to the three R's: reading, writing, and arithmetic. But the Chanel faculty was committed to increasing the number of minority students, which opened the door for me. I somehow got accepted and was awarded a partial scholarship.

Paying for the rest of my tuition was a tall hurdle for my mother, Elizabeth Archer, a single parent who worked as a bank teller at Cleveland Trust. She committed to cleaning office buildings when her workday was over to pay for it. Aunt Ann, my mom's sister who lived with us, promised to kick in a monthly amount as well. They both felt the sacrifices were worth it because the public schools were failing me.

My first week at Chanel was brutal. There was the cultural shock of suddenly being surrounded by a sea of white faces, which made *me* a racial minority for the first time in my life. Then I realized my classmates came from middle- to upper-middle-class homes, whereas I came from a household that could be charitably described as "working poor." I was also a religious minority because I attended a black evangelical church, which was miles apart in terms of worship style and doctrine from the buttoned-down Catholic community at St. Peter Chanel High.

"And now we'll hear from Bill Buchanan," Father O'Connell announced.

Bill, a lanky six-footer with Kennedyesque wavy hair, was a star tennis player and all-around good guy. He, too, spoke about the need to reduce the cost of prom and senior trips by holding all sorts of "fun fundraisers" to help defray the sizable costs.

As I sat there, gathering my thoughts, I realized I was being challenged. Running for class president—as a black kid attending a nearly all-white school—would test the Word of God, His promises, and all the things I had learned so far in life. This was the time to show the power of one man.

If I could do all things through Christ who strengthens me, as Philippians 4:13 promised, then I could understand how one man could take action, demonstrate faith, and show others the conviction bubbling in his heart. Was I going to embrace this opportunity to address my fellow students and inspire them to vote for me to become the first black student body president in the school's history? Or was I going to slink away and say this was too hard?

"And now, our third and final candidate, Ron Archer," Father O'Connell said.

I fastened the middle button of my blue blazer as I strode forward. Instead of standing behind the lectern, I unhooked the microphone and stepped in front of the podium.

This was my time to shine. I felt like a bucking bronc penned in a chute, about to be let loose. I didn't have to do this; I *was getting* to do it. I was as ready as Muhammad Ali was to fight Smokin' Joe Frazier in the "Thrilla in Manila," as ready as Kobe Bryant dribbling with his back to the rim, his Lakers team down by one and the final seconds ticking down.

This was my moment to show everything I had learned, both at Chanel and during my sixteen years of life. I wasn't nervous, but excited to display the gifts that God had given me. After a dozen rehearsals before my bathroom mirror, I was tremendously prepared to deliver my talk. I was also prayed up, so I was aligned mentally, physically, and spiritually. I knew the last thing my classmates wanted to hear was more fluffy talk about fundraisers to defray the costs of prom and class trips.

I looked at my fellow students, sitting in the bleachers to my right and my left, and cleared my throat.

"All of us have difficulties," I began in a soothing, modulated voice. "Some of us have alcoholic fathers. Some of us live in a divorced family. Some of us have issues with drugs and alcohol. Some of us are athletes who played with sprained ankles. Some of us stayed up all night studying for a test because there was so much turmoil in the home. We all have faced difficulties, but what makes a Chanel Man is this: He doesn't give excuses. Instead, he finds a way to be victorious."

I looked to my right, where hundreds of eyes were locked on me from the bleachers. I had their attention now. I pointed to one of my classmates, who was wearing his letterman jacket. Our school mascot was the Firebird.

"When we wear that jacket"—I took several steps closer to my classmate and pointed at him—"when you put on your school colors, you are a Firebird. This means failure is never final. This means failure is not an option.

"Now I understand that we all fail at one time or another. Perhaps some of you have failed academically. Maybe your relationship with your girlfriend failed. Maybe your team failed to win when it mattered most. But you know what? What happens in life is not final. When we fall down, we rise up from the ashes because we're Firebirds. We rise up because we will not accept failure."

The gymnasium was totally silent. I had everyone's attention as I told them the gist of my story—how I was a fatherless black kid from the inner city of Cleveland, a stutterer in elementary school, laughed at by kids in the schoolyard, and academically behind when I arrived at St. Peter Chanel.

"But when I was ten years old, a kind-hearted sixth-grade teacher named Mrs. Spears offered to meet with me after school to teach me how to overcome my stuttering. As we moved from breathing exercises to making certain sounds like *lee, la*, and *lo*—lee-lee, la-la, lo-lo—I built a new foundation of speaking without stuttering, brick by brick.

"Within months, I was transformed and could speak in public without stammering and stumbling over my words. No longer afraid to raise my hand in class, I became an excellent student. In fact, I was doing so well by the time I started my freshman year of school that my public school teachers told my mother that I needed the challenge of a top private school like St. Peter Chanel.

"Today I stand before you, humbled by the experiences of the last couple of years," I said. "I've learned that if you want to be great, then dare to tackle the difficult. That is why I seek your vote today."

I won the election by a landslide.

I believe God used the power of one man to make that happen.

Making History

Since the dawn of time, God has used one man to change and alter the trajectory of human history.

We can turn to the Bible and see how God has inspired a single man to respond to His call for transformational leadership. I'm thinking of individuals like Noah, Abraham, David, Paul, and the Son of God Himself, Jesus Christ, but I'm also thinking about you. Believe it or not, God wants to use you—a solitary, mortal man—to change the world around you for today and for generations to come. All it takes is for you to say, "Yes, Lord, here I am," and miracles are unleashed upon the earth.

The possibility of this happening is terribly exciting to me, especially in this unique time unfolding around us. In this post-COVID-19 world, where economic turmoil, rapidly changing social mores, and the way we personally interact look different every single day, I still believe that every man God creates has been born to achieve a particular mission.

Think about it:

The power of one man can change a country.

The power of one man can change a community.

The power of one man can change a school.

And the power of one man can change a family.

Think about the power of one man for a moment:

1. When God wanted to save humanity from total annihilation in the coming flood, He called out one man, Noah, to build an ark and preach about what he was doing for at least a hundred years.

2. When God wanted to create a chosen people who—after generations—would give birth to the Messiah, He called out one man, Abraham, to leave his mother and father and go to an unknown land.

3. When God wanted to save His chosen family from famine and starvation, He called out one man, Joseph, through a dream, to become their leader and savior.
4. When God wanted to put the tribe of Judah on the throne of Jerusalem to bring forth the Messiah, He called out one young man, David.
5. When God wanted to save the world from sin and condemnation, He became one Man to redeem all men (and women, of course) back to Himself.
6. When God wanted to spread the Gospel to the Gentiles, He called out one man, Paul, to preach, write, and plant churches throughout Europe and Asia Minor.

Throughout history, God has chosen one man—not a committee, not a group, and not a partnership—to do the work He wants to do. I call this the Law of Purpose.

Throughout history, every man whom God calls receives a divine message. I call this the Law of Inspiration.

Throughout history, every man God uses learns how to use God's transformational methods. I call this the Law of Effectiveness.

Throughout history, every man who uses God's methods becomes a magnet. I call this the Law of Magnetism.

Throughout history, every man who becomes God's magnet attracts more men, which builds a movement. I call this the Law of Multiplication.

Finally, when this movement gains collective momentum to achieve the God-ordained mission for generations, what I call the Law of Sustainability kicks into gear.

I believe He has great work ahead for each and every one of us. All you have to do is be aware that God has a **mission** that He wants you to fulfill. There's a mission for your existence. There's a mission behind why you are here. Jeremiah 1:5 (NIV) says:

Before I formed you in the womb I knew you,
before you were born I set you apart;
I appointed you as a prophet to the nations.

Samson had a mission to deliver Israel from the oppressive, pagan rule of the Philistines.

David had a mission to unify the twelve often-fractured tribes of Israel to become a great military power.

Solomon, David's son, had a mission to build God's temple in Jerusalem.

John the Baptist had a mission to prepare the Jewish people for the coming Messiah.

The Apostle Paul had a mission to preach the Good News in places where people had never heard of Jesus Christ, the Son of God who came to this earth and died for our sins so we may have eternal life.

Knowing that God has a mission for you can give you a life full of meaning and purpose.

Second, God gives each man a **message** to share with others. Since we're imperfect creatures, each man's message comes from his mistakes, his failures, and his brokenness, but out of that mess, a godly message of hope, redemption, restoration, motivation, and inspiration is forged. I like to say that where there's no mess, there can be no message.

Third, God gives you His **methods**, and those methods are always counterintuitive to the way the world does things. There's a reason God says, "For my thoughts are not your thoughts, neither are your ways my ways" in Isaiah 55:8 (NIV). His ways are almost always paradoxical, when you think about it.

Love your enemy.

The first shall be last, and the last shall be first.

Whoever wants to save their life will lose it.

God's methods go against the human mind. We want our revenge, served cold. We want to hate those who hate us. We want to hit back when we've been tagged. But that's not the way He wants us to go through life. His method is to love others as you love yourself.

After God gives us a mission, a message, and His methods, He makes us a magnet to draw both people and resources closer to Him to achieve the mission He's set forth for all of us. I've seen it happen time and again to myself and to many others: people will start coming to you with goods, with books, with land, with money, and with opportunities to fulfill His mission.

A great example is what happened to David and Jonathan in the Bible. First, a little background. We learn in 1 Samuel that David was the youngest of eight sons, born at a time when Saul was king of Israel. But God rejected Saul as king because of his halfway obedience and sent a prophet named Samuel to find the next leader of His chosen people. Samuel's search took him to the family of Jesse. When he met the family, he assumed that God would look at the oldest son of Jesse and anoint him as the future king. When Samuel listened to the Lord's voice, however, he was told that one of the sons was not there. The person he was looking for was the youngest boy in the clan—a shepherd boy out in the field with the sheep. He would be the next king.

Becoming king became David's mission.

To everyone's surprise, Samuel anointed David. It wasn't long before Saul was tormented by a spirit that could only be calmed by music. David happened to be skilled with the harp, so his nimble fingers played soothing melodies that proved to be just what Saul needed. But think about what this meant: A shepherd kid was able to serve in Saul's court and witness what running a kingdom looked like. He was given important errands to do, including running food to his brothers, who were part of Israel's army camped across the valley from the hated Philistines.

David heard Goliath dissing God and decided he'd take on a giant that everyone feared. We all know what happened: David slew Goliath with a rock from his slingshot, landing a smooth stone right between his eyes. When Goliath went down, Israel's army gained courage and routed the Philistines.

Who witnessed this incredible victory?

From a safe viewpoint, Saul and the son who he thought would be heir to his throne, Jonathan, watched this great victory unfold. This only goes to show you that when God calls you on a mission, two kinds of people will appear in your life: mentors and tormentors.

Saul would torment David and embark on manhunts to kill him. Jonathan, meanwhile, was a mentor to David. He drew him in like a magnet and "became one in spirit" with David (1 Samuel 18:1 NIV). Jonathan gave him his sword, his robe, his time, his teaching, his support, and his love.

You, too, can become a magnet to others. There isn't anything strange about that because Jesus says, "You are the light of the world." Light has a magnetic pull to it because the sun, which is light, has so much density and energy as well as a gravitational pull. When you're filled with the presence of God to fulfill a mission, He gives you His light, which makes you a magnet. I like to call that *magnetism* or *gravitas*, which draws people and resources into your orbit for one reason: to achieve your mission.

Drawing people and resources closer to you shouldn't be done to give you a big head, reap awards, make you rich, or make you powerful. Instead, it's done to help make you more effective.

◆   ◆   ◆   ◆

Why am I writing *The Power of One Man*?

I want one man—you—to know how significant you are, how valuable you are, and how important you are to God. We are unique, dynamic, and special creatures. Consider this from Psalm 8:3–6 (NIV):

When I consider your heavens,
the work of your fingers,
the moon and the stars,
which you have set in place,
what is mankind that you are mindful of them,
human beings that you care for them?
You have made them a little lower than the angels
and crowned them with glory and honor.
You made them rulers over the works of your hands;
you put everything under their feet.

Look how special God is and how we've lost that! And in many cases, we've lost the significance of how God views us. We've lost the significance of what our purpose is, how beautiful we are in the eyes of God, and how God redeemed us through one man: Jesus Christ.

I want you to be inspired by the message that one man can make a difference, although I understand that you may be alone. You may be depressed. You may be broken. You may be divorced. Suicidal. Alcoholic. Abused. Lost your job. Lost your sense of direction and purpose.

A turnaround can start when you embrace your manhood from God's point of view, not man's point of view.

That turnaround can start today. To help you get started, I will address several key issues that leave many men feeling like they are missing in action and prisoners of war.

◆   ◆   ◆   ◆

Discussion Questions

1. Was there ever a time when you had to step out of your comfort zone? What did you do to overcome feelings of self-doubt?

2. Philippians 4:13 (NLT) says, "For I can do everything through Christ, who gives me strength." Do you know that the Holy Spirit longs to strengthen you? What can you do to be strengthened by the mighty hand of God?
3. Have you had any miracles happen in your life? If so, what was the most recent one?
4. Have you ever gone on a missions trip to a foreign country? If so, what was the best thing you learned?
5. Do you know anyone who is a light to others? What makes that person special in your eyes?

2

MIAs and POWs

I start with a question: Did you grow up in a fatherless home?

If you did, that means your father was missing in action. Through no fault of your own, you became a prisoner of war, so to speak, because you never had an affectionate, supportive, and involved father contributing to your social development, academic achievement, sense of well-being, or feelings of self-esteem.

I grew up without these key parenting elements because I was raised both without a father and with a father in the home, which takes a little explaining. I'll start at the beginning by declaring that there was no dad cradling me in his huge arms following my birth on June 15, 1963, in Cleveland. The reason why is because my mother, an unwed seventeen-year-old at the time, didn't know who my father was.

How was that possible? At the tender age of sixteen, my mother, Elizabeth Peru, went into the sex trade out of desperation. Her father, a black man who'd immigrated from Cuba, was missing in action; he was imprisoned at the Ohio State Reformatory, a maximum-security state prison in Mansfield, on a trumped-up charge. At the same time, her mother, Greta, a white daughter of German immigrants, was recovering from the removal of a cancerous tumor in her brain—a life-saving surgery that also resulted in the loss of her left eye.

During Greta's long recovery, my mother—the oldest of seven children—had to assume many of the child-rearing duties in the home as she was starting high school. With no visible means of support and so many hungry mouths to feed and shelter, Elizabeth said yes to working in the world's oldest profession, easily justifying what she was doing: she was helping her family survive. After a year of "turning tricks," she became pregnant, one of the hazards of earning money the way she did.

Despite several attempts to abort me, I survived and came into this world prematurely—a month early. I weighed four pounds, two ounces. My lungs were underdeveloped, which impacted my breathing. I'm told that I battled pneumonia right off the bat. My skin coloration—I was caramel-colored—wasn't healthy. I was definitely a baby suffering from Fetal Alcohol Syndrome (FAS), although the condition wouldn't have a name until 1973.

My mother was a child having a child, so my grandmother looked after me most of the time. After a few months of getting back into shape, Elizabeth returned to the skin trade. This time, though, she thoroughly hated what she was forced to do and wanted a way out.

An exit plan presented itself in Dick Archer, a man fifteen years her senior with a solid job as an apartment manager and real estate investor. Their relationship was basically a trade-off: Mom and I could move out of my grandmother's house and live in one of the apartments that Dick managed, and her suitor would have some arm candy and someone to share his bed.

From the time we moved in with Dick—I was three or four years old at the time—I was told that he was my father. As any innocent preschooler would do under those circumstances, I called him "Dad" and treated him, well, like he was my father. Why would I do anything else? That's all I knew as a preschooler through my early elementary school years.

When I got a little older and started grade school, Mom told school authorities a fib: my name was Ronaldo Archer. Hearing my teacher say "Ronaldo Archer" during roll call cemented in my mind that Dick Archer really was my father.

I couldn't understand why he didn't want anything to do with me, however. I saw other dads in the neighborhood playing catch with their sons after they got home from work or shooting hoops together at the local playground. Mine? All he was interested in was plopping down in his easy chair and cracking open a cold beer while he flipped through the newspaper. He never wanted to teach me how to run and catch a pass, swing a baseball bat properly, or make a layup. One of my dreams was to ride on his tall shoulders one day, but he never hoisted me high above him.

As I entered grade school, he never hesitated to verbally and physically abuse me. I'm not sure which was worse: the lash of his tongue or the back of his hand.

What really set him off was when I wet my bed. Nobody told my parents that bedwetting was often a sign of psychological problems and emotional distress, but during my elementary school years, I was an emotionally troubled kid who stuttered in the classroom and was mercilessly made fun of in the schoolyard. I also had an underdeveloped bladder since I was born a month prematurely. Put everything together, and it's no surprise that I'd wake up with wet sheets in the morning, which ticked off both my parents—especially my dad. His volcanic temper would explode.

"Boy, how many times do I have to tell you not to wet the bed!" I'd hear after every episode.

And then I'd brace myself for the slap to the head or a heavy push to the ground, followed by several strong smacks to my butt. He'd really give me a good thrashing.

His physical abuse of me was nothing like what my mother had to endure, however. I witnessed horrible fights between my parents all the time. Sometimes Archer showered my mother with a torrent of verbal abuse and could be quite cruel. "You have nowhere to go," he'd taunt her. "Without me, you'd be back on the streets."

Other times he skipped the verbal tirade and punched her with clenched fists.

Whack..."Take that, bitch!" *Whack*.

One time, I heard my father taking out his frustrations upon my whimpering mother from my upstairs bedroom. I felt helpless to come to her aid because I knew he would turn on me in a heartbeat. He was too big, too strong.

And then I heard the front door slam. There was quiet in the house. My father had left to cool off, maybe at a local bar.

I tiptoed downstairs and found Mom on the living room couch, holding her battered face in her bloody hands. She looked up, tears coming from her eyes. One of them was black from taking a direct hit. Blood dripped from a corner of her mouth. Mucus filled the jowls of her face.

"I'm sorry, Mommy." I sat next to her and wrapped an arm around her shoulder.

"It's over," she said softly. "That's the last time he steps inside this house."

And just like that, the "father" in my life disappeared and divorce proceedings started since the state determined they had a common-law marriage. We got to stay in our house, but without Dick Archer's income, we were living off food stamps and eating potato soup.

Startling News

It was right around this time that my mother sat me down and told me the stark truth: Dick Archer was not my father, and she didn't know who my real father was.

That was hard for a fourth-grader to take in. The news staggered me and left a gigantic hole in my heart. A longing grew within me—a longing to know who my real father was.

Where did I come from?

Who is my dad?

How come he doesn't want to know me?

I could never put these unanswered questions out of my mind.

What happened is that I became another statistic in the epidemic of fatherlessness that has swept this country a lot longer than COVID-19 has—and with far greater consequences, I believe. Fatherlessness can be associated with nearly every societal ill facing our country's children, including:

- Poverty
- Drug and alcohol abuse
- Poor physical and emotional health
- Inadequate educational achievement
- Crime rates
- Early sexual activity
- Teen pregnancy

According to the U.S. Census Bureau, children in father-absent homes are almost four times more likely to be poor, and 44 percent of children in mother-only families live in poverty, compared to just 12 percent of children in married-couple families.[1]

Fatherless children are at a dramatically greater risk of drug and alcohol abuse, according to the U.S. Department of Health and

Human Services. In terms of physical and emotional health, a study of two thousand children three years and older without a father or a male role model in the home found that they experienced significantly greater external and internal problems than children living with married biological parents. These behavioral problems lead to a greater probability of committing a crime and going to prison.[2]

Fatherless children are also likely to abuse alcohol and are twice as likely to suffer obesity and drop out of high school. Children without stable relationships with their dads are more susceptible to depression, more likely to become drug addicts, and more likely to demonstrate delinquent behavior. Consider these sobering statistics from the U.S. Department of Justice:

- 63 percent of youth suicides are from fatherless homes
- 90 percent of all homeless and runaway children come from fatherless homes
- 85 percent of all children who show behavioral disorders come from fatherless homes
- 80 percent of rapists with anger problems come from fatherless homes
- 71 percent of all high school dropouts come from fatherless homes
- 75 percent of all adolescent patients in substance-abuse centers come from fatherless homes
- The vast majority of mass shooters grew up in fatherless homes[3]

There is an epidemic of destruction that comes from one man not being a man. And the ripple effects throughout the culture are cataclysmic. They truly are. Boys are particularly vulnerable and are in serious trouble. As authors Warren Farrell and John Gray explain in their book, *The Boy Crisis*, boys are experiencing a crisis in education and falling behind girls in the classroom, a crisis in mental health with attention-deficit/hyperactivity disorder (ADHD) rates exploding, and a crisis of purpose. The root of all this is fatherlessness.

These days, twenty million children—or more than one child in every four—live without a father. Broken down by race, the problem of fatherlessness becomes especially acute.

According to government statistics, 72 percent of African American children are born to unmarried mothers, followed by Hispanics (53 percent), whites (29) percent, and Asians (17 percent).[4] This is where I want to speak a little bit about the African American male experience because the tragedy of fathers missing in action (MIA) and their prisoner of war (POW) children is far greater for African Americans than for other races.

Let's start by going back hundreds of years to when Africans sold other Africans to European and American slave traders back in the seventeenth, eighteenth, and nineteenth centuries.

Slave owners were determined to break down the family unit and create reproductive breeding stables so they would never run out of slaves on the plantation. What slave owners did to keep up their number of slaves was to determine who the strongest "buck" was and train him to breed—not to be a father. If his qualities of strength, stamina, and endurance made better field hands, the slave owners would treat him like a stud, much as owners do with racehorses.

Throughout each new generation, too many African male slaves learned their value wasn't in being a father, being responsible, being present, or being a protective covering for their families. Their value came from making as many kids with as many black women as possible. That's where their accolades came from; that's where their value came from.

This perverse situation went on for some time, from when the first slaves came to America in 1619 all the way up to the end of the Civil War in 1865. Then we had a hundred years of Jim Crow laws and segregation, in which adult black males were called "boy" regardless of their age.

Hey, boy. Get over here and shine my shoes.

That was your name—Boy. You were not equal to a white man. You were not equal in society or the eyes of the law.

Then a major challenge to Jim Crow came with the Civil Rights Movement of the 1960s. Dr. Martin Luther King Jr. and his group, the Student Nonviolent Coordinating Committee, staged "sit-ins" at restaurants that refused to seat black people as a way to "integrate" the establishment.

More often than not, they got a lot of food dumped on their heads. A better strategy would have been to bring together a collection of churches and their black men and build their own restaurants rather than going to somebody else's place and begging them to take their money.

But that was a tactical decision that can be debated. Even though the Civil Rights Movement set this country in the right direction, the formation of the welfare system under President Lyndon Johnson's "Great Society" initiative in the 1960s has turned out to be even more destructive to the black family.

The major component of the welfare system, which was developed with input from Dr. King, was basically this: if a woman has a child and wants or needs assistance from the government—money for housing, food stamps, and all sorts of Aid to Dependent Children benefits, including health care—then Uncle Sam will provide all of these benefits, *as long as the father is not in the home.*

Think about the ramifications of this policy decision, which illustrates the law of unintended consequences: if the father of the child lives with the mother, either as a married spouse or as a live-in boyfriend, the mother of the child loses all her government benefits, or most of them.

So the black woman with one, two, three, or more kids has to make a decision: *Do I accept this black man—who might be working as a shoeshine boy, a car-wash guy, a plumber, or a Walmart manager—instead of the benefit I'm getting from Uncle Sam? Or do I reject him and become a welfare mom?*

The latter is the choice that a majority of African American women have chosen for the last fifty years, which has led to the demolition of the two-parent home in the black community. This is why 72 percent of black children are born out of wedlock today.

Let that number sink in, because we know that 80 percent of our social ills come from raising children in single-parent homes. These children grow up to become POWs, not realizing they are in bondage. They grow up with the mindset that they are free—free from responsibility, free to do their own thing—but they are really not.

They are like the elephants in the circus.

◆　　　◆　　　◆　　　◆

Now I understand that circuses with performing elephant acts are banned in many major cities across eighteen states (because of the training regimen I'm about to describe), but I would imagine that sometime in your lifetime you saw a gigantic elephant do tricks under the big top.

He stands up on a ball. He turns around. He dances. He does whatever the trainers tell him to do, and then he gets a handful of peanuts for his trouble. It's amazing how a little man with a black top hat and a small whip can make this gigantic beast obey and do anything he wants.

The elephant is the largest land animal on Earth—and the strongest. Doesn't the elephant know he can break free at any minute and the trainer won't be able to stop him? So what keeps the elephant in slavery and in bondage?

Training circus elephants begins when they're very young and after they are separated from the herd. The trainer puts ankle bracelets around all four legs. The bracelets have spikes facing inward. The trainer takes each bracelet and attaches it to a chain that's embedded in some kind of concrete hole.

Whenever the baby elephant tries to break free, the spikes pinch into his skin and into the nerves, creating severe pain. The harder the elephant tries to break free, the more pain he experiences. The harder he tries to get back to the herd, the more pain and agony he experiences. So he learns to try a little less and a little less and a little less. The less he tries, the less pain he feels. This process is called "learned helplessness," meaning this is when the elephant learns to be helpless.

He learns not to try.

He learns not to give any effort.

He learns that he's not going to be free.

When this elephant grows into a formidable two-ton animal, he really believes there's no way to break free. All the trainers have to do is keep one bracelet tied to one of the front legs as a reminder: *You're not going anywhere. If you try, you're going to feel pain.*

This means the elephant accepts that it's not big and powerful. This learned helplessness, also known as arrested development, means that the elephant may weigh four thousand pounds but sees itself as a small calf.

It grieves me to say that I've know many men who've been through significant trauma or excruciating emotional events that have crippled them like circus elephants. They see themselves as boys. They see themselves as incapable. They see themselves as inadequate.

Oh, they certainly look like men. They talk like men. They walk like men. But emotionally and psychologically, when they're under pressure, they respond like young adolescent boys. They are the products of learned helplessness and arrested development.

We all know men who have great abilities and amazing talent, but we've also seen them act like little boys. They have tantrums. They can't control their impulses. They can't control their sex drives.

Look at former heavyweight boxing champion Evander Holyfield. He had 11 children by 6 different women. The $230 million he earned over a 26-year career is gone, along with his 3 wives. So is his 109-room house.

Hollywood star Eddie Murphy is the father of ten children by five women. Ex-NFL cornerback Antonio Cromartie has fourteen children with eight women—four of them coming after he had a vasectomy! His child support payments in the hundreds of thousands of dollars each year have sucked his bank account dry.

I could list a dozen more examples, from boxer Mike Tyson (eight children by three women), to NFL wide receiver Terrell Owens (four children by four women), to the NBA's Calvin Murphy, who has a whopping fourteen kids with nine women. They had great abilities and talent in their chosen sports, but they acted like little boys in the areas that really count.

Those with learned helplessness see themselves as victims and adopt an attitude of entitlement. *You owe me for the way I was born. I'm not responsible for my actions, nor am I accountable because the system owes me a solid. The world owes me. You owe me.*

I saw this when I was working as a pastor in the Cleveland area. Every Monday, we fed the homeless at our church. We would stock a pantry with food, sign up volunteers to cook, prepare tables so everyone would have a place to eat, and invite the homeless to come in.

Every Monday afternoon, they would line up outside the church for a free meal. Some of our volunteers would sing songs and read Scripture while they were served a well-balanced plate of food such as lasagna with green beans and a salad or spaghetti with meatballs and collard greens.

We also had boxes of clothing available, and people donated old bikes and other sorts of useful things. I'll never forget the time, though, when we were serving food and one homeless guy approached us with a Styrofoam plate in his hand. As a square of lasagna was placed on his plate, he got pissed.

"What the hell is this shit?" he demanded.

"Pardon me?" I said.

"I said, 'What do you call this shit?'"

"It's lasagna," I replied.

"I don't like no damn lasagna."

"Wait, wait, wait. Hold on here," I said, holding up the line. "You're homeless. You have no food. We're volunteering our money and our labor to prepare this meal for you."

"I don't care!" And then I watched him heave the plate over my shoulder and into the wall behind me.

This was not an isolated incident. This happened time and time again. It was like the homeless people felt entitled to some other type of meal, something more grandiose—like steak and lobster?

I talked to other pastors who said, "Oh, yeah, Ron. Happens all the time. If you serve something they ate yesterday at another shelter, they cop an attitude."

This is what learned helplessness and the psychology of entitlement look like. It's the foundation of self-destructive behavior where the homeless bite the hands that literally feed them, where teen girls are having babies out of wedlock, where teen boys are dealing drugs and getting caught up in gangs, and where young adults are making trouble.

It's heartbreaking to see this happening in our next generation, but understandable when you consider that the rational part of a teen's brain isn't fully developed until age twenty-five or so. That's why you see thinking like this:

- *I'm so unique that the rules don't apply to me*
- *I can take that drug and not get addicted*
- *I can have sex and not get pregnant*
- *I can steal from that liquor store and not get caught*

- *I can skip school and still make a million dollars playing football*

Then we have something called "terminal uniqueness" sweeping through the minds of young people. They think they're the only ones who've gone through problems in life. They think they're the only ones who grew up without a father, which gives them license to act out.

Because men tend not to talk with other men and fail to open up, this terminal uniqueness leads to even more self-destructive behavior.

◆   ◆   ◆   ◆

Let me turn the corner now to white men and the challenges facing their ability to be the one man they'd hoped they'd be. The fact is, we have a lot of middle-aged white men without college degrees living in the "suicide belt" in the western United States.

In states like Arizona, Colorado, Idaho, Montana, Nevada, New Mexico, Oregon, Utah, and Wyoming, rates of suicide have been sky-high in recent years. Wyoming has the highest suicide rate in the nation with thirty suicide deaths per one hundred thousand residents, more than triple the rate found in New York and New Jersey.[5]

The typical man who takes his life is between the ages of fifty-five and sixty-five and comes from a blue-collar background. These men are carpenters, plumbers, welders, truck drivers, ranch hands, and custodians. I understand how it can be mentally tough to be in your late fifties and living in a caretaker's unit behind a multimillion-dollar vacation home at a fancy ski resort.

But returning veterans from Afghanistan suffering from post-traumatic stress disorder (PTSD) are also at high risk for suicide, as well as those who worked in tourism or the hotel industry and grew frustrated with the low pay and the seasonality of their jobs. They are taking their lives in inordinate numbers.

This societal development deserves attention because these are the men who built this country but feel left behind, unappreciated, and blamed for every *-ism* in America. They are committing suicide at a rate 30–40 percent higher than any other group—black men, black women, white women, Hispanic men, and Hispanic women.

I bring up the twin trends of arrested development for black men and the spiraling rate of suicide for white men because both groups feel that society has left them behind and that their lives no longer carry any value. They also get tossed aside the minute their bodies start breaking down.

Back problems, joint pain, and knee replacements often result in tremendous pain. When these men see their doctors, they walk out of the examination room with a prescription for OxyContin, a powerful opioid that's been called a "love drug" or "cuddle chemical."

Taking these pills allows them to go back to work or cope with their pain, but these opioids are highly addictive. Users quickly reach the point where they can't function without their daily dose.

But doctors generally won't write any more prescriptions after three months, which means these men have to buy more OxyContin somehow or go through withdrawal symptoms. So they talk to some friends.

Don't worry about it, man. I know a guy. He can get you some-thing for five dollars a bag that does the exact same thing. It's called heroin. You can sniff it, you can snort it, you can smoke it, or you can shoot it.

And that's why we have POW men dying from drug overdoses in crazy-high numbers. In 2018, a total of 67,367 people died from drug overdoses, according to the U.S. Centers for Disease Control and Prevention, and two-thirds of them were males.[6]

So imagine being a man of honor all your life. You've been a hardworking man. And then you become middle-aged, and society begins to turn its back on you. They say that your values are irrelevant, old-fashioned, and no longer valued. They say your masculinity is "toxic."

Your kids are turning against you. You're going through a divorce. You have all kinds of physical ailments. And now you find yourself either hooked on alcohol or opioids.

You don't talk to anybody about it. You don't go to an AA meeting. You don't go to "recovery groups" because you've learned the value of rugged individualism. Real men don't cry.

Real men don't reach out for help.

Real men pretend they're OK.

I met a man just like that one time. He was worth fifty million dollars, but his family deserted him, saying he was too old-fashioned and too rigid in his beliefs. I'm scrunching a lot of years together and skipping a lot of details, but as his life spun out of control, he took his hound dog, his 20-gauge shotgun, and went for a drive around the lake, intent on killing himself.

"I was about to pull the trigger when my dog looked at me with a face that said, 'What about me?' And I thought: *Someone cares about me, even if it's a dog.* That was enough for me to back off from the precipice, which is why I'm talking to you today."

But what about the man of middle- or upper-class means who has made mostly good decisions and/or has been raised right by good parents in an intact home? They are some of the most clueless men on the planet because they think they have it all. Many find out they don't, that their lives don't have purpose beyond the dollars or toys. They also pull the trigger or find addictions to numb their own pain.

These are the folks I'm writing *The Power of One Man* for. If you're broken, missing in action, or a prisoner of war, I want you to understand that God loves you, that you have value, and that you have purpose. Since the beginning of time, God has taken broken men, men who feel left behind, and men with sketchy backgrounds to change the world. For instance:

- Jacob was a deceiver who became the "father" of the Israelite nation
- Joseph was a slave who saved his family from famine
- Moses was a man-slayer and a shepherd in exile when he was called upon by God to lead the Hebrews out of bondage to the Promised Land
- Gideon was a farmer who delivered Israel from the Midianites
- Jephthah was the son of a prostitute who delivered Israel from the Ammonites (and someone I strongly identify with)
- Ezra was a scribe who led the return to Jerusalem and wrote some of the Bible
- Matthew was a despised tax collector who became an apostle and the author of one of the four Gospels
- Peter was a fisherman who became an apostle and leader of the early Church

God uses all sorts of common people to do His work. He knows the power of one man. You are part of God's creative design for this broken world. You can change yourself, your family, your community, and your world.

◆   ◆   ◆   ◆

So I understand how MIA fathers produce POW men. I understand how the absence of a father in the home is the root of kids' academic problems. I understand how it's nearly impossible to understand the power of one man if you never saw it modeled growing up.

So what can you do if you grew up in a fatherless home and feel like you're a walking POW?

Here are several points to consider:

Let Jesus be a father to you. The Lord offers Himself as the ideal father to those without earthly fathers. Psalm 68:5 (NLT) says: "Father to the fatherless…this is God, whose dwelling is holy." Psalm 27:10 (NLT) reminds us: "Even if my father and mother abandon me, the Lord will hold me close."

If you had a father missing in action, the Lord offers to fill the role of a father. He taught His followers to address God as Father. You can cast all your worries on Him and call out to Him when you're in trouble. Let Him teach you through His Word what was never taught to you at home.

Hang out with men you respect and look up to—and let them take you under their wing. When I came to faith in Christ at a summer church camp at the age of eleven, Pastor Eddie Hawkins was the dynamic preacher who presented the Gospel and changed my life.

Let me describe Pastor Hawk. Built like a fire hydrant, this stout, powerful preacher commanded attention in his erect bearing, in his careful diction, and in his mesmerizing presentation. I could not keep my eyes off him every time he took the pulpit at the summer camp.

I attended Pastor Hawk's church every Sunday after that, and I'm sure he noticed the young boy sitting up front, looking up and hanging on his every word. Flash forward a few years to when I dropped by his office during my junior year of high school.

"What brings you here, Ron?" Pastor Hawk said as he showed me to a seat.

"Pastor, I was wondering if I could check out a couple of your Bible commentaries." I looked to the right, where a bookshelf filled with volumes stood next to the wall.

"I don't see why you can't do that," the pastor replied. "But I don't usually have kids like you asking to borrow my Bible commentaries. So what's interesting you?"

I shifted in my seat. "Well, I like reading the observations and teachings of well-respected Bible scholars after I'm done with my homework."

I think I could have knocked over this former Golden Gloves boxer with a pin feather. But you know what? After that day, Pastor Hawk saw something in me. From then on, he invested in me—and I welcomed that investment. I listened when he described what went into preparing his sermons, I saw his reliance on prayer, and I noticed the way he treated the love of his life, Sister Norma Jean Hawkins (to use an honorific common in the black church).

After studying several biblical commentaries and discussing what I learned with him, Pastor Hawk stunned me one afternoon. "Ronaldo, the elders want me to lighten my load around here. I believe God has an anointing on your life to preach. I'd like you to take on the Sunday night services for me. Can you do that?"

Could I? I was thrilled to give preaching a try, with some pointers from Pastor Hawk. Looking back, I don't know why Pastor Hawk would pick a fatherless sixteen-year-old to share the Word of God with five hundred church members, but he did.

The lesson is that when you gravitate toward being a godly man, God can do amazing things—if you let Him.

Stop using your past circumstances as an excuse not to stand on your own two feet. OK, you got a really, really bad break growing up—your father wasn't around. That happened to me as well. I had some really rough moments growing up; I'm sure you did as well.

I understand that a "victim" mindset is common these days, especially in the black community. But I have to point out that everyone gets overlooked, ignored, attacked, abused, and cheated during their lives, which means we're all victims at one time or another.

Wallowing in your victim status may feel good in the short term, but it's not the way to go through life. Injustice is as old as time itself.

Can you take ownership of and responsibility for your needs? You start by asking yourself what's important to you. Once you've made that determination, ask yourself: *What do I need to do to make this happen?* Make a plan and get busy taking care of what's important to you.

Finally, turn your focus to helping others. It's amazing how your perspective changes when you drop what you're doing and help others in their time of need. Bye-bye victim mentality and hello good vibrations. As weird as this may sound, the more you may have been deprived, the more you have to give because you have life experiences that need to be shared, need to be learned from. I've long believed that you cannot become a transformational man until you've had a transformational experience.

Life has always been 10 percent what happens and 90 percent how you respond to it. You can have an attitude of gratitude and live with hope, joy, love, and inspiration if you see yourself as someone who comforts the disturbed and disturbs the comfortable. I'm fond of saying that you can turn your pain into power, which is the perfect antidote to seeing yourself as a victim.

Everything you've gone through in life is a down payment on your destiny. I can illustrate this by holding up a lotus blossom: a beautiful, aromatic plant that grows best in the darkest, filthiest manure. The dirtier the manure, the more wonderful the fragrance.

And that's how life should be. Sure, your feet may be stuck in dark manure at the moment, but God is working to bring forth a beautiful flower with a pleasing aroma to others.

Let Him grow you.

There's no better way to experience the power of one man.

In my next chapter, I'll unpack a strategy to restore men based on five action points.

◆　　　◆　　　◆　　　◆

Discussion Questions

1. Did you grow up in a fatherless home? Describe how that impacted your life in ways great and small.

2. Fatherlessness is associated with higher rates of poverty, drug and alcohol abuse, and higher rates of incarceration. What do think of the staggering statistics regarding these societal ills? Do they make sense to you?

3. Do you know any young or middle-aged men who are products of learned helplessness and arrested development? What are some common characteristics of these men?

4. Were you surprised to learn about the high rates of suicide for men in states like Wyoming, Montana, and Arizona? What do you think is causing so many despondent men to end their lives?

5. Have there been times when you felt like a POW—imprisoned by how your life has turned out? What advice shared in this chapter resonated with you?

3

A Strategy to Restore Men

After I came to faith in Christ at a church camp when I was eleven years old, something deep in my heart told me that Jesus could be the father missing in my life.

I really wanted to go to church and learn more about the Jesus Christ that Pastor Hawkins preached about so eloquently. If the doors to Good Shepherd Baptist Church were open, I was there. Monday nights started the week with a kids' Bible-memorization program. Pastor Hawk led a worship service on Wednesday nights, while our youth group met on Friday nights, which was a good way to keep teens off the streets. Sundays were practically wall-to-wall church: we began with Sunday school at 9:00 a.m., followed by the main worship service that began at 10:30 and ran way past lunchtime, and a Sunday night service at 6:00 that was shorter but no less engaging.

I was like a sponge in my pre-adolescent and early teen years, sitting under Pastor Hawk's teaching and soaking in God's Word. What

I noticed about Pastor Hawk's sermons was how he laid out a section of Scripture and used it as a launching pad to make three points about what the Lord was calling us to.

I loved the rhythm of Pastor Hawk's teaching as he worked through his exegesis (a word I certainly didn't know at the time). But no one could explain, explicate, or expound on the Bible like Pastor Hawk could. That was another thing he liked to do—use alliteration as a way to open up the Word of God to his listeners. He'd talk about not feeling discouraged, disheartened, or deficient but having the power, preeminence, and peace of Jesus in your heart. He'd say that God wants three things from every believer: our surrender, our service, and our supplication, along with a reminder that we are to love God with our head, our heart, and our hands.

His alliterative references have stuck with me to this day and are a reminder that folks in the pews tune in much better when they hear repeated sounds at the beginning of words. The use of alliteration creates rhythm and mood, helping listeners and readers focus their attention on an idea or emotion.

In honor of Pastor Hawk's three-point way of preaching, as well as his use of alliteration, here's my five-point strategy to restore men and tap into God's power:

- Be present
- Be attentive
- Be affirming
- Be consistent
- Be committed

If you want to take on the challenge, if you want to become a change agent, and if you want to be the man you've dreamed of, then you should regard each of these action points as foundational principles. Keep them in mind as you move forward in life. When you do, you'll firmly grasp the power of how one man can change himself, his family, and the world around him.

And now to my first point:

1. Be present. When I was a young pastor, one of the things I really struggled with—even disliked—was making hospital visits, especially to see elderly folks. I felt as though I hadn't lived long enough to be of any help to them. What could I possibly offer to those who had so much experience in living?

Consequently, I would overprepare and study things like how we can be healed through the "stripes of Christ," but however much I studied, making the trip to the hospital or hospice room was pure drudgery for me.

One time, I met an older lady who was part of our church. When she was sick and I made a house call to her, she perceptively noticed that I was nervous in her presence.

"Do you understand what your value is to me?" she asked from her bed.

"I'm not sure that I'm understanding you," I said.

"The fact that you care enough to show up, to sit with me and hold my hand, and that you have enough love to take time out of your busy schedule to come see me is tremendous," she said. "Your presence is a blessing to me."

That day I was reminded of the power of presence, the power of being visible and available. These days, my mother has been hampered by stage-three dementia, which means she doesn't remember what happened yesterday, doesn't know what day it is, or what month we're in. But she is in the moment. We can go for walks, and I'll cook dinner for her and comb her hair, and she can still play her favorite game, Connect Four.

Mom is having so much fun, despite her mental condition. She is liberated, unlike us, and she is free from the pain of the past and the fear of the future. All she has is the present, so she lives her life fully in the now because in her mind, her reality is always in the now.

That's a good reminder of how we should live and be present. God said, "I am," which means all there will ever be in your life is what's happening right now. You can't change the past, and the future is yet to come. All you can do is impact the present, so be kind now. Be loving now. Be forgiving now. Make good decisions now. Be prayerful now. Reconcile with others now.

Being present also means showing up for duty. You can't be missing in action or still be stuck as a POW. This is the time, to use a catchphrase that's current in our culture, to "man up."

This term was popularized in a series of Miller Lite ads in the early 2010s that shamelessly used male gender stereotypes. Perhaps you can recall the dippy TV spots in which a thirty-something guy, hanging out with friends in a bar, orders a light beer from a hot-looking, know-it-all female barkeep.

"Do you care how it tastes?" she asks.

"Nah, just give me what you got," replies the clueless male. "I really don't care."

The cute bartender acts all put-out while she pops the lid on a bland no-name brew. "When you start caring, I'll give you a Miller Lite," she says with the confidence of someone who knows her light beer.

That's when the camera pulls back and shows the dude either wearing a pink skirt, holding a "man purse," or wrapping a woman's scarf around his neck. "Man up," intones the baritone voiceover at the end of the thirty-second spot, "because if you're drinking a light beer without taste, you're missing the point of drinking beer."

While that's worth a chuckle, I see "manning up" as being ready to respond to the call of duty. When it comes to taking responsibility for where you're going in life, the choices you make in your interpersonal relationships, and your desire to serve God, you need to be present and accounted for.

I've come across too many Christian men who have been AWOL because they either are afraid or don't know how to step up and lead in their families, homes, or churches. I had to face those fears when I embarked on my campaign to get elected as student body president at Chanel High. At the time, I was well aware that I was not white, Catholic, affluent, or connected—but I was present and ready to tackle the moment.

Because I was present, I took that risk. Winning the election and becoming student body president at an all-white private high school illustrates an important principle about the power of one man. What I did was turn orthodoxy, which is when a person believes the right things, into orthopraxy, which is when a person does the right things. The Bible teaches that if we truly have the correct beliefs, then our behavior will align with them. That's the power of one man in a nutshell: living out your faith in a way that affects the way you live and impacts those around you. That can only happen when you are present and accounted for.

We need the presence of men in our culture and in our churches. My heart grieves when I'm preaching and I look out at the audience and see many more women than men in the pews. My heart grieves when I read that women outnumber men in world missions. My heart grieves when I see it's the women organizing the food drive, not the men.

We need men to man up and be present in the home. Men give children insight into what masculinity should look like and how men think, an overlooked aspect of childrearing these days. They can stress rules, playing fair, and explaining the consequences of right and wrong. They can prepare their children for the challenges of life. They can call the heart of a man out of a boy, but fathers need to be close enough to their sons to do that. They need to be present in their children's lives.

We know, from psychological research of families from all ethnic backgrounds, that a father's affection and increased family involvement promotes children's social and emotional development. But have you ever noticed that you can take your kids fishing, to a ballgame, or Home Depot on a Saturday morning and never say more than a few words? Even though you're saying next to nothing, they're still watching you closely, and they see how you interact with them and others. That's why being present means everything to your children.

When you're spending time with them, they sense there's no judging, no putting them down. You don't have to be some great teacher or preacher to impact your children on behalf of the Kingdom. You just have to be there.

But none of those great things can happen if you're missing in action. That's why you need to be present—today, tomorrow, and for years to come.

2. Be attentive. There's no way to sugarcoat this observation: men have difficulty in being attentive. In fact, the prophet Isaiah took note of this more than 2,500 years ago:

> No one has ever heard,
> No one has paid attention....
> —Isaiah 64:4 (GW)

Men—often described as "clueless" by their wives and girlfriends—brush over the importance of being attentive without realizing that paying attention is a form of intimacy. You build intimacy with loved ones by being attentive, and a great way to do that is by asking good questions, which shows that you're engaged with that person.

Have you ever had a conversation like this with your wife?

"What do you want to do tonight, honey?"

"I don't know. What do you want to do?"

"I don't know either. Don't you have any ideas?"

"It really doesn't matter to me. Whatever you want to do will be fine with me."

The more attentive husband will ask a deeper question than "What do you want to do tonight, honey?" An exchange like the following will sound better to her:

"What's the most fun we've ever had on a date?"

"Oh, the time we rode our bikes and you took me to that little bagel shop for lunch."

"Well, would you like to do that again?"

You can show that you're being attentive by being cognizant of the difference between good questions and *great* questions, which also shows that you're present in your spouse's life. Here are some key components of great questions:

A. Use questions that can't be answered with a simple yes or no. Nothing puts the brakes on a conversation like asking questions that can be answered with one word. You want to engage the mind, the personality, and the opinions of your loved one.

B. Know why you're asking a question. The reason I say this is because the tone of a question will get more of a response than what's being asked.

C. Avoid leading questions. Great questions should be two-way streets, not dead ends. The best way to avoid asking leading questions is to wholeheartedly listen to your loved one's response, which is a great example of being attentive.

D. Don't ask a good question at a bad time. An attentive man knows that the best time to ask questions is not when *he* wants to ask but when his loved one is ready to respond.

E. Use *would* instead of *could*. Asking "Would you do that for me?" sounds a lot better than "Could you do that for me?"

To help you move from being clueless to being attentive, consider these examples:

- When she says, "We need…" what she really means is, "I want…"
- When she says, "Do what you want," she really means, "You'll pay for this later!"
- When she asks, "How much do you love me?" she really means, "I did something today you're really not going to like."
- When she complains, "I'm fat," what she's really saying is, "Tell me I'm beautiful."
- And finally, when she says, "Are you listening?" it really means, "Too late. You're dead!"

There's another angle to being attentive: your attentiveness to your fellow man can help you help *him* if he's going down the wrong road. You can point out, in a loving way, that he's not taking the right path or making good choices.

I call this "confronting with care." You do this by focusing your comments on the issue at hand or the behavior you're seeing—not on the person. You want to do your best to maintain your personal objectivity because the minute you attack a man, you put him on the defensive. Any chance for a positive outcome will be eradicated.

Another thing you can do to maintain others' self-esteem is to avoid the use of the word *but* in your conversation. What I mean is that everyone involved in social discourse has been taught to say something nice—before lowering the boom.

Hey, you know I like you. You're a great guy. We've been friends a long time—but there's a problem we have to address.

When this happens, it creates something known as *cognitive dissonance*. It's like you're saying to the person, "I really like you… but I don't."

The next time you need to say "but," I recommend that you try inserting the words "next time" along with the advice you want to impart.

You know that I like you, Ron, so the next time you give a speech, think about how you can touch people with a personal story.

In these situations, avoid saying things like, "I liked your speech, Ron, but you can do better." Instead, speak plainly and tell them how they did as honestly and positively as you can. I always say that well-spoken feedback is the breakfast of champions.

3. Be affirming. If you talk to a lot of men and they get real with you, they'll tell you their fathers put them down. They'll tell you they were overly criticized by their dads. They'll tell you that their fathers told them they'd amount to nothing.

All those things happened to me when Dick Archer was part of my childhood. One of my ways to cope was to bang my head against the headboard of my bed. I would thump my head again and again and again after being put to bed. I did that because I was trying to forget the memories of the horrible things my father said about me, cutting remarks like, "You're destined to live on the streets, boy, just like your worthless mother. You've got no chance in life."

So I banged my head in an attempt to escape my surroundings. That's how I fell asleep every night. My spirit was broken.

Many men go through life feeling broken and unaffirmed, but very few will volunteer that information. The fact is, too many men don't have anybody—including their wives—with whom they feel comfortable talking. They don't have any friends to whom they feel they can reveal everything. But when you develop relationships with other men, you give them a golden opportunity to open up and express themselves freely to you, which gives you an opportunity to affirm them.

We could all use affirmation in our lives, but it's not something you can ask for. I've found that if you want affirmation—and who doesn't?—then start by affirming others. Never underestimate the power of your own influence, even as one man. Whether you're in formal leadership or not, people will never forget the impact of your lifting, affirming words.

A great way to affirm others is by asking them this question: *What are you most proud of about yourself?*

I'm always amazed by the variety of answers I receive—and the lack of responses. Too many men can't think of *anything* they're proud of about themselves, while others are so full of themselves that they bend my ear for the next half hour about the award they received at work or their kids' exploits on the playing field.

Most of the time, though, men were beaten down in childhood, just like me. Even though regrettable incidents may have happened in your life, I urge you to make yourself proud by looking for ways to build up others. Here are some ways to do that:

Practice giving spontaneous praise. There's no reason to save up your kind words for a special occasion. This is especially easy to do with social media these days. Compliments for a job well done or an anniversary or birthday on Facebook or Instagram let recipients know how special they are—and the rest of the "friends" in cyberspace get to read your compliments.

Look for ways to give encouragement. People need affirmation the most when they're going through a rough patch. Encouraging words will fill their sails with hope.

Notice the good things they're doing. If someone goes out and grabs a box of donuts for the break room, go out of your way to pay a compliment just as they went out of their way to be thoughtful and bring a treat for the morning coffee break.

It really doesn't matter if you're a vice president, a division head, a foreman on the shop floor, or a rookie on the assembly line: you can affirm others by reminding them that they're born by divine design. Share Genesis 1:27 (NIV):

> So God created mankind in his own image,
> in the image of God he created them;
> male and female he created them.

There are fewer more affirming Scriptures than that passage.

4. Be consistent. In January 2020, I made a commitment to fast for twenty-one days, something I've done frequently to start a new year. I typically fast for ten days drinking water mixed with lemon juice, and then for the next eleven days, I do a version of the "Daniel diet," which is eating vegetables and raw foods.

This time around, though, I wanted to do something different. I decided that before I started the fast, I would spend seven days consistently before the Lord, devoting an extra hour every morning and every night to Bible study and prayer. I call this concept "abiding in the Lord." The idea is that if a man is really going to change, he must be in the presence of the Lord. He must be abiding.

I was determined to be consistent in my added prayer and study time before I embarked on my long fast. I'm telling you that once I went seven days with an extra hour in the morning and the evening in the presence of God, my mind and my soul were changed. And the fasting was far easier this time. In fact, I was able to fast on water and lemon for *fifty* days in early 2020. I remember going on a TV show during that time and talking about the power of fasting and prayer through consistently applying the principles of abiding and how that made the difference for me. I spoke about how the Lord said to me, "Not by might or power, but by My Spirit."

I couldn't believe how easy the fasting was because in the past, it had always been a struggle for me, as it is for nearly everyone. But this time around, it felt as easy as breathing because I consistently decided to abide in the presence of God. When you're consistent in your prayer life, consistent in your study of God's Word, and consistent in your devotion, it's a transformative experience for the heart, the hands, and the habits. Consistency is the key to excellence in anything you do. When you're consistent, you will reach what you're striving for.

Consistency should be something that everyone wants. Consistency develops routines and momentum. Consistency forms habits that become almost second nature. If you've developed the habit of reading the Bible each morning, then you know how it feels a bit off to *not* sit down with God's Word before you start your day.

One time, I saw a great mentoring program start in a certain church, but after a while, it ran out of steam and stopped. When that happened, I daresay that the kids were worse off than before they started being part of that program.

Kids need consistency—we all do. I've always said that consistency allows for reciprocity, which allows for transformation. When consistency stops or is cut short, transformation isn't going to happen.

People value consistency. It removes uncertainty and leads to trust, which, in turns leads to being able to influence others on behalf of the Kingdom. Author and pastor John Maxwell said, "Small disciplines repeated with consistency every day lead to great achievements gained slowly over time."

When it comes to being consistent, keep these points in mind:

- **Consistency makes you relevant.** The church that ended the mentoring program before it gained traction stopped being relevant to those kids. Everyone likes predictability in their daily lives.
- **Consistency maintains your integrity.** If you say one thing to one person and something else to another, people will either get confused or figure you're just another huckster.
- **Consistency keeps you focused on your goals.** Your ability to hold yourself accountable grows and solidifies when you finish tasks consistently and with excellence.
- **Consistency improves your relationship with God.** We know that God is always working in our lives, but if you don't spend time in His Word, which allows you to tune your heart to His voice, you will miss the occasions

when He speaks to you. If you want to grow closer to God, be consistent. Find time to be alone with Him every day without distractions.

5. Be committed. When I was a junior in college, I helped lead an effective Bible study for around 250 students every Wednesday night—so large that we held it in a big auditorium. Each week, we seemed to add to our numbers.

Then I was hired to be a summer counselor for the Upward Bound program, a federally funded education program that helps students overcome class, academic, and social barriers to higher education. One of the young women who worked with me was not a Christian. She was a smoker, a drinker, a party person, and extremely bright. She also walked around angry and cynical while attacking people. She did not believe in God, but when she heard about how successful I'd been on campus—I had been elected to the student body government and was leading a large Bible study—she could tell that I had been transformed. She became a bit softer.

I noticed this and committed to being a light in the darkness for this young woman. One time when I was walking past her dorm room, I poked my head inside and said, "There are three things you can be in life when it comes to God. You can be curious, you can be convinced, or you can be committed. Committed is tied to one word—obedience. It's not just talking about it, or thinking about it, or dreaming about it. It's about being obedient and doing what God's Word says to do."

An hour later, she visited my dorm room. "I'm curious about what being committed looks like," she said.

We chatted some more, and she agreed to meet me in the cafeteria the next day, where I opened my Bible and went through the plan of salvation. We talked about how there is none righteous before God, not even one (Romans 3:10), how we've all sinned and fallen short of the glory of God (Romans 3:23), and how the wages of sin is death, but the free gift of God is eternal life in Christ Jesus our Lord (Romans 6:23).

That day, she committed herself to God. She had this very dynamic boyfriend who was a football player and part of a fraternity. They were having premarital sex. After giving her life to the Lord, she told him, "From this day forward, no more sex until we're married."

"Why?" was his first question.

"Because I've committed myself to Jesus. He is my husband, and I cannot betray Him."

"Who taught you this nonsense?" he demanded angrily.

"Ron Archer."

That's when I received a visit from this powerful football player who was ready to tackle me to the ground and beat me up. "My girlfriend is a fanatic, and now we can't have sex anymore because of your stupid teaching," he said. "I want you to stay away from her because you're crazy!"

I attempted to defuse the tense situation. "What I taught her was the truth, and I'm not going to change it."

He left in a huff and sought out his girlfriend. He demanded to know if they were going to go back to the way things were before.

"Listen to me very closely," she said. "You're making me choose between you and Jesus, but I'm committed to this new life. I've stopped smoking, stopped drinking, and stopped having premarital sex with you. If you force me to make a decision between you and Jesus, it's not even close. I'm choosing Jesus, so goodbye."

A week later, this guy went back to her and said, "What must I do to be saved?"

You see, he was torn apart to learn that this young woman was more committed to Jesus than to him, but that all changed when he gave his life to Christ. His name was Joe Wilson, and he's been in ministry ever since that day thirty-five years ago. He also married that woman named Dierdre. Joe's been a pastor over many churches, a leadership trainer for John Maxwell, and the author of a book about the power of prayer. That's the power of commitment. That's the power of going all in.

Let me stress the difference between casual commitment and making a strong commitment through telling a barnyard story involving a breakfast of ham and eggs, which is the breakfast I grew up with.

As you look at your plate, I'd say the chicken was casually involved with your meal. But the pig was personally committed.

So let me ask you this:

Are you "involved" with God or "committed"?

Are you "involved" with your church or "committed"?

Are you "involved" with your community or "committed"?

And lastly, are you "involved" in your marriage or "committed"?

Regarding the last question, love isn't dependent on feelings or emotions but on a deep and abiding commitment to one another, no matter how you may be feeling in the moment.

Commitments are powerful because they influence how you think, how you act, and how you handle things when times get tough. I remember when I made a commitment to attend new membership classes at Good Shepherd Baptist Church after I came home from camp, where I had come forward to accept Jesus into my heart after the invitation by Pastor Hawk. The new membership classes took place over eight weeks, which involved a commitment of getting to church on time at 9:00 a.m.

I remember the commitment I made to memorize the Bible in my teen years—hundreds of Scriptures. Thankfully, I had a photographic memory and a thirst to commit God's Word into my heart, but you know what? This is where I learned that God, the Father, was committed to me. The fact that God Almighty was a protector, a teacher, a guide, a mentor, a coach, a leader, and someone who would never leave me or forsake me carried great meaning for me. In other words, I knew that God the Father was committed to me.

◆   ◆   ◆   ◆

The reason why I love writing about the power of one man is because you are valuable. You are important. You are significant, and the devil wants you to believe that you really don't amount to a hill of beans in this world. That's a lie from the pit of Hell—because if one man says yes to God, amazing things can happen.

Here's what I mean: If a child comes to faith first in his family, there's a 3 percent chance that his family will also come to faith, according to LifeWay Christian Research. If a woman or mom commits herself to Christ, there's a 15 percent chance that her family will too. But when a man says yes to Jesus first, there's a 93 percent chance that the *entire* family will come to know Jesus.[1]

I was the first to commit my life to Christ in my family, which I've already told you about. All these years later, I can confidently say that *every single person* in my immediate family has come to a saving knowledge of Jesus and accepted Him as Savior.

I'm humbled that He used me that way, which is why I can boldly declare there's power in what one man can do on behalf of the Kingdom.

I understand that you may not feel worthy or up to the task. We have all fallen short in our lifetimes, and I know I have as many flaws as the next fellow. There have been many times when I wished I had taken different steps at certain times in my life.

But I was willing to allow Him to use me—one man—in a way that has glorified Him. In becoming His vessel here on Earth, I used God's power to find my destiny, which is still being written.

There are those who have gone on before me who have great stories to share on the power of one man. As I promised in my opening chapter, I want to share how biblical heroes like Noah, Abraham,

Moses, and Paul—who all had their flaws—overcame their shortcomings to impact future generations.

They each demonstrate the power of one man.

◆　　　◆　　　◆　　　◆

Discussion Questions

1. How would you grade yourself regarding "being present" and "manning up" with those closest to you?
2. What are some other ways to ask others great questions besides asking questions that can't be answered with a simple yes or no?
3. When was the last time that someone affirmed you or encouraged you that has stuck with you? What did that person say that was so memorable?
4. Have you ever fasted? What was that experience like? How long did you fast? What was the enduring benefit?
5. What could you do to become more consistent in reading your Bible and getting plugged into a church or a men's group? Would you say you're "involved" with God or "committed" to God?

PART II

The Power of God's Men

4

One Man's Story:
Noah and His Ark

Maybe you've heard the old joke:

Need an ark? I Noah guy.

We can all chuckle, but the story of Noah, one of the best-known narratives in the Bible, is incomprehensible if you stop and think about it. Really? A flood covering the earth's surface and even the world's tallest mountains? But that's what Scripture tells us:

> For forty days the floodwaters grew deeper, covering the ground and lifting the boat high above the earth. As the waters rose higher and higher above the ground, the boat floated safely on the surface. Finally, the water covered even the highest mountains on the earth, rising more than twenty-two feet above the highest peaks.
>
> —Genesis 7:17–20 (NLT)

The basic story of Noah and the ark is that as the children of Adam and Eve populated the earth—living hundreds of years, I might add—people continued to overstep God's boundaries, which is a nice way of saying that they were "utterly wicked," "corrupt," "violent," and "totally evil," according to various translations of the Bible. We can only speculate on how bad people were back then, but it had to be notable and universal because Scripture describes Noah as the "only blameless person living on earth at the time" (Genesis 6:9 NLT).

Talk about the power of one man.

It's interesting to mull over this thought: If Noah hadn't "walked in close fellowship with God" (Genesis 6:9 NLT), what would God have done to save a race that had totally gone off the rails only ten generations removed from Adam?

But because Noah was available and blameless before Him, God decided to hit the reset button.

After God told Noah that He'd decided to destroy all living creatures—wiping them out because they had filled the earth with sexual sin, violence, and every form of evil—He directed him to build a large boat from cypress wood and waterproof it with tar, inside and out. The dimensions of the barge-looking vessel were unworldly: three hundred cubits long (around five hundred feet), fifty cubits wide (around eighty-five feet), and thirty cubits high (around fifty feet). To paint a more modern picture, this vessel was a football field and a half long and nearly five stories tall. NASA could lay three Space Shuttles nose to tail on the ark's roof.

So how did one man get this wooden monstrosity built? Scripture tells us that Noah had three sons—Shem, Ham, and Japheth—so they surely helped him with the scaffolding, sawing the wood, and piecing together the boat. Noah certainly couldn't go down to the union hall and hire a crew of carpenters to help him.

The Bible doesn't specifically say how long it took Noah and his sons to build the ark, but when Noah is first mentioned in the

Bible, he is already five hundred years old. When he enters the ark, he's six hundred years old, so it might have been around one hundred years.

Whatever the length of time, Noah worked on the ark and preached to all who dropped by to mock him for building a humongous boat. Yes, Noah preached. We know that because in 2 Peter 2:5 (NIV), Noah is referred to as a "preacher of righteousness."

So here's what I want to point out: After a hundred years or so of building and preaching, Noah did not have one convert!

No one listened to him and said, "You know what? Noah could be right. God could judge us for our wickedness. So what do I have to do to get right with God?"

Which leads me to ask you a series of questions:

- Could you be that faithful for that long while being mocked and ridiculed?
- Could you continue to work on God's behalf for so long without seeing any results for your efforts?

Pondering these questions reminds me of a story about a young man who traveled to a decadent, sinful, and lascivious city so that he could preach against the wickedness found among the citizens. Standing on a soapbox in the middle of a crowded park, he spoke with such sincerity and passion that a crowd gathered around him.

Each day he returned to the same spot, and the crowds got bigger and bigger each time he preached. But he slowly realized that nothing was really changing in the city, even though the crowds remained large.

Preaching every day took its toll. Over the years, his voice weakened and his hair turned gray. The crowds began to dissipate. Eventually, he found he was speaking to almost no one.

A young boy walked by one afternoon. He saw an old man, now with a gray streak running through his hair and a gray beard covering his face. He was still talking about love, faith, salvation, redemption, and holiness. The boy stopped to listen. When the old man was done, the boy said to him, "Sir, my dad said you've been preaching here for twenty years, but if you look around, nothing's changed. Why do you keep talking? Why don't you stop, sit down, and retire?"

The old man stepped off his soapbox and walked over to a park bench, where he asked the boy to sit next to him.

"Son," he began, "when I first came here, I spoke because I really thought I could change the world around me. Now I speak so that the world doesn't change me. If I'm the only one left who believes in God and His promise of eternal salvation, then I'm the only one left."

One man. One commitment. One goal in life.

Can you be as committed when you don't see changes happening right away? Maybe you're stuck in a dead-end job or find yourself living in a part of the country that you vowed never to live in. Maybe you tried to lose weight for the umpteenth time and the ten pounds you shed came right back. Maybe today you don't see anything changing and have lost hope. But can you be as faithful as Noah, who built an ark without seeing one person converted over a hundred years?

This is a good time to think about your core values and beliefs. Do you believe what you see and what God has said? Do you believe what you feel and what God has promised? Do you believe what you observe and trust in God's future for you?

Everyone back in Noah's day thought he was crazy, just like all those who witnessed the young man standing on a soapbox in the middle of a park. But both men were faithful and willing to serve God without seeing immediate results because they were obedient to God's call on their lives.

◆   ◆   ◆   ◆

Noah was ridiculed for his obedience. If he had lived in our time, he would have been subject to a bunch of nasty memes. I can see one now: "Crazy dude builds giant ark for supposed flood that will never happen."

Yet his faith in doing what God directed him to do never wavered. In Hebrews 11:7 (NIV), we read:

> By faith Noah, when warned about things not yet seen, in holy fear built an ark to save his family. By his faith he condemned the world and became heir of the righteousness that is in keeping with faith.

It wasn't just the grace of God that saved Noah. His faith and obedience were the difference.

You see, faith and obedience go together. Faith can only be measured through obedience. Obedience is the visible expression of invisible faith.

Faith requires action. This is most difficult when God asks us to do something contrary to popular opinion or that includes a big risk. The question is no longer "Do I believe God?" but "Do I believe God more than my own reasoning or my neighbor's opinion? Am I willing to do what God asks of me, even when I don't fully understand it?" This is the kind of faith that expresses itself in obedience.

Grace is God's unmerited gift to us. It is the foundation of Noah's story and the core of our salvation. It is God's grace that delivers us from sin and brings us into His Kingdom. This is a gift that's available to anyone, but it's our choice to engage with it.

Noah's obedience has implications for our everyday lives. Whether you're aware of it or not, God has a plan for your life, your family, your workplace, and your city. He already has the building plans finished, and He's looking for people who will believe Him and express this faith through obedience. His Word is filled with commands, not because He is demanding or angry, but because He wants to outline His building plan so that you can live a thriving life that glorifies Him. This happens through the partnership of His grace as well as your obedience.

When God saved my soul while I was in grade school, He made it clear, as I grew older, that He wanted me to build an ark to save my family. That ark was my personal life. How I lived would allow my family to see the love, favor, and power of God.

My family was a motley crew—six aunts and uncles on my mother's side, as well as my mom's parents.[1] Not only did they not go to church, but they didn't even like church, which they thought was reserved for fools and hypocrites.

The hardest nut to crack was my grandfather, who would often say, "I hate white missionaries. They came with the Bible when my African ancestors had the land. One time, they asked the Africans to bow their heads and close their eyes to pray. When the Africans finished praying and opened their eyes, they had the Bible in their hands and the white missionaries had the Africans' land in theirs."

While simplistic, that's what my grandfather—a black Cuban immigrant—believed. And who could blame him? "Big Daddy," as I called him, experienced the worst of Jim Crow while working the cotton fields of Alabama in the 1930s. He witnessed lynchings and knew never to make eye contact with white people—especially white women. He went through life being called "boy," "nigger," and "coon."

Life improved when he moved north to Cleveland in the early days of World War II and found decent work in the factories, but when he married a white woman in 1944, he experienced a fresh wave of racism. Things were so bad that whenever he and Greta drove around, she had to sit in the back seat so that fellow drivers thought the black man behind the wheel was the chauffeur—not the husband.

And then Big Daddy went off to prison and Greta found herself in a battle for life with a cancerous tumor in her brain. Following her life-saving operation, Greta's father came to see her at the hospital. He was a big, tall, strapping German, an immigrant from the Old Country.

While at her bedside, he said this to her: "I'm sorry this cancer happened to you, but I want you to know why it happened—it's because you sinned against your family."

Greta nearly fell out of her hospital bed. "What do you mean?" she demanded.

"You married a black man," he replied. "Didn't I teach you that light doesn't have anything to do with darkness? So here's the deal. If you will leave your shame behind"—by shame, he meant her seven children—"we'll take you back to Germany. We'll take care of you, we'll love you, and you'll want for nothing."

Greta looked at her father, whom she adored. At one time she was a daddy's girl. After a moment of gathering her thoughts, she replied, "How can you only see color? These are my babies. I'm all they have. And you want me to turn my back on my children and turn them into wards of the state and go back to Germany? I could never do that."

"OK, but you're digging your own grave," her father coldly responded.

With that, Greta's father left the hospital room. When he returned home, he announced to the rest of the family that Greta was excommunicated from the family. They were never to talk of her or see her again—a practice called shunning, which is widely used in the Amish community. This was the ultimate social distancing.

From that moment on, Greta was treated as though she were dead. Her father even made a simple oak coffin and had his wife and other children deposit all of Greta's clothes and belongings in it. A grave was dug in the backyard, and the coffin was lowered into the ground. The memory of her was also buried that day.

When that horrible story was passed on to Greta's children—that their parents were a cursed couple because light and darkness can't be together—it made sense that my uncles and aunts regarded religion with bitterness, anger, rage, and rebellion.

So consider how I found myself, as a young Christian, facing all of this family vitriol toward God, toward the Church, and toward religion. My mom would actually get angry with me about my fanatical commitment to Good Shepherd Baptist Church and Pastor Hawk's preaching.

A typical thing she would say on a Sunday morning, after I came down the stairs dressed in my Sunday best with shined shoes, was, "Mop the floor."

This meant having to skip breakfast since there wasn't enough time to do both. I'd fetch the mop from a closet, fill a bucket with water and bleach, roll up my pants legs, and start to mop.

"Oh, no, no," she'd say. "You're afraid of water."

That's when she'd dump the whole bucket all over the floor, which created a mess and a ton more work.

I didn't complain, although I knew her outburst meant I would go to church smelling like a new cologne called Clorox. The reason I didn't cop a bad attitude is because the only thing that was going to save my mom was how I treated her—not doctrine or dogma. My life had to be full of the nine attributes of the Holy Spirit: love, joy, peace, patience, kindness, goodness, faithfulness, humility, and self-discipline.

These were the key ingredients to building an ark for my family. My ark was my obedience. My ark was my humility. My ark was my forgiveness. My ark had to reflect the life of Jesus.

When I got to driving age, Mom would hide my car keys so I couldn't go to church on Sunday mornings. "Let Jesus find them for you," she'd say in a huff.

But what softened my mom and my sister, Crystal, day by day, hammer by nail, was the life that God was constructing for me. I was bringing home "A" report cards, quarterbacking the football team, and becoming the first black student body president of my high school. I was asked to fill in for Pastor Hawkins on Sunday nights.

During my senior year of high school, as I was preaching one Sunday night to lighten the load for Pastor Hawkins, I looked up and saw my mom walk into Good Shepherd with Crystal on her arm. I had never seen my mom darken a church door.

My sister, a year earlier, had given her life to Christ and was joining me on Sunday mornings at Good Shepherd. But my mother? She was still a tough nut to crack.

That evening, I planned to preach on Rahab the prostitute, but I didn't know my mother was going to be there! I had to pray really quickly for direction, and I felt like the Lord was telling me to ahead with my planned sermon.

The story of how God used a prostitute to help the Hebrews to a tremendous victory at Jericho and how she then became the ever-so-great-grandmother of Jesus touched my mother. When I made the altar call, she came forward. We both wept when Mom made her way down the center aisle to make a public demonstration of her decision to place her trust in Jesus Christ. The emotions that welled in my chest were nearly impossible to contain. My mother was saved!

A few years after that amazing event, I led Big Daddy to Christ before he died. The same is true of my grandmother, whom we called Grannie, as well as all my aunts and uncles. I shared my testimony with my cousins, and they became believers as well.

All because of the ark the Lord directed me to build.

◆   ◆   ◆   ◆

When the storms of life hit, I call this God's classroom. This is His way of preparing you to become a man of God, and He does that through three phases that I want to introduce to you. They are:

- The set time
- The mean time
- The appointed time

The **set time** is when God calls you and reveals the blueprint of the ark He wants you to build, the life He wants you to lead, the ministry He wants you to conduct, or the business He has compelled you to launch. Do you want to build an ark using the instructions of God like Noah did—with no steering wheel, no rudder, no lookout station? Or do you want to build the RMS *Titanic*, a ship so mighty that its captain, Edward John Smith, boldly declared, "Even God himself couldn't sink this ship"?

We all know that Noah's ark survived the greatest storm in the history of humanity—forty days and forty nights of torrential rains. The *Titanic*, unfortunately, didn't survive her maiden voyage in 1912 when she struck an iceberg and slipped into the icy waters of the North Atlantic, taking more than 1,500 souls with her.

Noah followed God's blueprint to the last cubit with a desire to exalt God, not himself. Noah knew that he had a set time to build what God wanted him to build because God knew what was coming.

Everyone I'm going to write about in this book had a set time. Besides Noah, Abraham was called by God to start a nation of His chosen people. Joseph had a dream. Moses stood at the burning bush.

David was anointed by Samuel. Paul had his Damascus Road experience. If you believe in the power of one man, realize that God can reach out and knock on your door today. He can appear to you through a song, through a preacher, through a sermon, or through a crisis, but I can assure you, in one way or another, God will reveal Himself to you.

Look at your set time with exhilaration and excitement, as a time of destiny and purpose. And when God calls you, He could give you a preview of what's to come. Consider what He told Abraham in Genesis 15:5 (NLT):

> Then the Lord took Abram outside and said to him, "Look up at the sky and count the stars if you can. That's how many descendants you will have!"

God told Moses that He had chosen him to lead the Hebrew nation to the Promised Land, a land flowing with "milk and honey."

Let the set time motivate and inspire you, push and challenge you, prepare and propel you.

Next comes the **mean time**, which is mean...not pleasant. I'm referring to a great time of struggle, when God allows life to pull you in the opposite direction of the very thing He's called you to do. It's a time of doubt and confusion, a time of bewilderment. Perhaps everything God has shown you has turned into a shambles. That happened to Abraham when he was told to leave his homeland and be a stranger in the land of Canaan. That happened when Moses had to leave Egypt as a fugitive. That happened when Joseph was thrown into a pit and then sold into slavery.

Everyone gets tossed into a dark, dreary pit sooner or later. When that happens to me, I remind myself that P-I-T also stands for "prophet in training." Everything that goes forward in God's velocity must first be pulled backward. An arrow in a bow must go backward before it shoots forward. A rock in a slingshot must be pulled backward before it goes forward. Even Jesus had to descend before He ascended.

So the question becomes this: What releases you out of your pit? As long as you're whining and complaining, making excuses for your decisions and behavior, God will say, "You're not ready yet."

An example is when a silversmith boils silver in a cauldron. If he lets the silver boil too long, it burns. If he takes the silver away too soon, it becomes cloudy. There's just the right time when the silver is ready to come off the fire, and it's when the silversmith can see his flawless reflection in the pot. When he sees himself with clarity, then he knows it's time for the silver to be released from the fire.

When God can see Himself in you, He knows you're ready for the next stage, which I call the **appointed time**.

This is when the ark is built, and God gives you a message that becomes a magnet that draws your family two-by-two into His holy plan of salvation and redemption.

◆   ◆   ◆   ◆

There's an interesting ending to Noah's story: the Bible reveals that after the Flood, he got so drunk that he got naked and passed out. So why did God include that story in His Word?

I'll use Martin Luther King Jr., the civil rights activist of the 1960s, as an example. Dr. King's compassion and ability to lead and inspire others were unbounded. His ability to maintain his public equilibrium was remarkable. Yet Dr. King had major flaws—infidelity, and at times a painful inability to acknowledge the pain that those around him experienced.

The Bible and our world are filled with flawed humans who experience and inflict pain and turmoil on others. Like Noah, we are flawed and heroic, noble and base, all woven into one. As we embrace our humanity, let us learn from our mistakes and confront our pain so that we can emerge stronger and wiser. And as we delve further into the characters in this book, let us use their lives to understand our own lives better.

You see, God never calls the qualified. He qualifies those He calls. God uses imperfect people to reach other imperfect people, who, by His Holy Spirit, become His perfect work.

Noah was not perfect. He had his flaws just like any one of us. But what he did was tremendous; in building the ark for all those years, he demonstrated the power of one man.

I urge you to build your ark. There are three traditional roles that men can play to help define their manhood as Ark Builders:

1. The man's ark or life should provide for his family's safety. Spiritual safety from the wrath of God happens when everyone in the family has been introduced to the grace of Jesus Christ for salvation. Take them down the Roman Road of salvation.

Emotional safety happens when everyone feels safe to share their honest thoughts and concerns without being condemned or threatened for speaking their minds.

Environmental safety happens when you try your best to create an ark that protects your family from sexual predators, abusers, bullies, and threats. It's proven that when a dad is not around, many children who are left unprotected are vulnerable to sexual abuse. That happened to my mom and to myself because we didn't have fathers around to create an environment of safety.

2. The man's ark or life should create stability. Stability means providing the economic resources to meet the needs of the home, by being a man who is worth following. Scripture says that a man who does not provide for his family is worse than an unbeliever and has denied the faith (1 Timothy 5:8 NIV).

We all can do something to contribute to the financial stability of our homes. Over the years, I have worked some pretty interesting jobs to provide stability for my family as an Ark Builder. I worked at a greenhouse growing trees, pumped gas at a service station, cleaned office buildings, and worked as a farm hand. Sometimes you do what you gotta do to stabilize the family.

3. The man's ark or life should create serenity. We are to provide an ark or a life that brings peace to our families and communities. Jesus said, "Peace I leave with you; my peace I give you. I do not give to you as the world gives. Do not let your hearts be troubled and do not be afraid" (John 14:27 NIV).

This means peace in the midst of the storm, calm in the middle of the hurricane. This means no overreaction to mistakes, no raging when upset, no condemnation when mistakes are made, but acting with a calm, mature, and responsible character under pressure.

The attributes of safety, stability, and serenity are what we receive when we spend time in devotion, prayer, worship, and conversation with God every morning. When we stay in the presence of God, we receive by proximity His love, joy, and peace.

When we are saturated by God's love, joy, and peace, we are able to give patience, kindness, and goodness to others on a consistent basis. When we act in this way to others, we become faithful, humble, and self-disciplined.

Men, it works. We must learn how to become human beings rather than human doings. We have to do something to have something, so let me ask you this:

Was there ever a time in your life when you experienced a broken, shattering situation that brought you to your knees? You thought you had it all together. You thought you were flying high, but you realized that you were drifting away from God. You were focusing on being a human doing, not a human being. You got caught up in your own accolades, your own adoration, and found that you didn't need God as much.

But then you entered into a significant emotional event—a storm—that almost killed you. What did you learn from that experience? What did you have to face that helped you realize that you had to give control of your life back to God? The Bible says there is a path before each person that seems right but ends in death (Proverbs 14:12 NLT), so use these broken experiences to remind yourself that you need God every moment of the day and every step of the way. That's how you become an Ark Builder.

Sure, it may take a lifetime to get there, as it did for Noah, but once your ark is built, you can withstand the storms of life. If there's anything we've learned from 2020, it's that everybody needs a place for protection from a storm. Whether it's a financial setback, a relationship squabble, a marital argument, or a health issue, everybody at some time in life will face a huge storm.

So have your ark ready.

You'll be glad you did.

◆   ◆   ◆   ◆

Discussion Questions

1. Noah spent at least a hundred years building the ark, yet no one outside his immediate family believed it was going to rain. When God calls you do something that nobody believes in, how do you push through?

2. What kind of boat are you building with your life—an ark or the *Titanic*? How do you know when a call is coming from your ego or is truly of God?

3. When you face storms or significant trauma, how do you transcend and overcome them?

4. When you fall, how do you start all over again? What have been the steps that you've taken in the past that worked for you?

5. God gave Noah the mission of rebuilding humanity. Do you need to rebuild your marriage? Rebuild your health? Rebuild your finances? What are you going to do? How are you going to start?

5

One Man's Story:
Abraham, from Pimp to Prophet

M y family and I were driving to the park recently when *Game of Thrones* came up in our conversation.

Having never read the books or seen the HBO show, but figuring the reviews I'd read and the trailers I'd seen gave me all the information I needed to know, I pontificated, saying, "*Game of Thrones* is popular only because it's all about sex and violence."

To which my son, Chris, responded, "Sex and violence. Sounds like your favorite book, Dad—the Bible."

I was embarrassed because he had a point. The Bible is full of stories about fornicators, adulterers, prostitutes, polygamists, ethnic cleansing, fratricide, infanticide, and other forms of cruel activity.

The Old Testament, in particular, is full of sexual violence. We read of rapists, pimps, and other perpetrators of sexual exploitation. The Bible, one might conclude, is not so different from *Game of*

Thrones...or even watching the nightly news. Every day we seem to hear about sexual assaults on college campuses, in the military, and even in churches. Sadly, many of us are no longer shocked when we hear such horrific reports.

This reality makes studying sexual violence in Scripture all the more pressing. The Apostle Paul said all of Scripture, including what we might consider the R-rated stories of the Old Testament, is God-breathed and useful for teaching and training us in righteousness (2 Timothy 3:16–17).

It's not that we should skip over such stories, but we tend to use euphemisms when telling them. We don't pay close attention to the details, and as a result miss what the biblical authors intended to communicate.

Stories of prostitutes, adulterers, and fornicators, as well as sexual predators and human traffickers, teach us profound lessons about God and His grace. One of the greatest stories along these lines involves Abraham, considered the patriarch of the world's three major monotheistic religions: Christianity, Judaism, and Islam.

For Christians, the genealogy of Jesus Christ can be traced to Isaac, Abraham's son. In Judaism, it's understood that the Jewish people descended from Isaac, born of Abraham's wife, Sarah. In Islam, Abraham's firstborn son, Ishmael, born of the Egyptian servant girl Hagar, is viewed as a fulfillment of God's promise; the Prophet Muhammad is his descendant.

But here's another thing I want you to know: Abraham, this revered father of the faiths, was a serial liar and a pimp who turned into a prophet.

Let's begin by reviewing Abraham's backstory. We know that his father was Terah. Joshua 24:2 (NLT) tells us:

> This is what the Lord, the God of Israel says: "Long ago
> your ancestors, including Terah, the father of Abraham and

Nahor, lived beyond the Euphrates River, and they worshiped other gods."

According to Jewish tradition, Terah was a successful idol salesman in the local marketplace, faring well financially and socially.
Extrabiblical legends tell us that Terah once went away on a journey,
leaving Abraham in charge of the stall where the clay idols were on
display. In a moment of conscience, he took a wooden stick and shattered all the idols except the largest one. Then he placed the stick in
the hand of the largest idol.

When his father demanded to know what happened, Abraham
told a white lie: "Oh, Father, the small idols got hungry and started
fighting for food, which caused the largest idol to get angry and break
them into little pieces."

That's the moment when Abraham broke with idolatry, but not
the last time he played loose with the truth, as we will soon see.

Whether the story of the idols is true or not, God knew what He
was doing when He made Abraham an offer he could not refuse:

> Leave your native country, your relatives, and your father's
> family, and go to the land that I will show you. I will make
> you into a great nation. I will bless you and make you
> famous, and you will be a blessing to others. I will bless those
> who bless you and curse those who treat you with contempt.
> All the families on earth will be blessed through you.
> —Genesis 12:1–3 (NLT)

That had to be pretty heady stuff to hear. People didn't talk about
leaving a legacy back then, but who wouldn't want to be known for
forming a great nation and becoming a famous person in the annals
of history? And the material blessings that God was talking about had
to be the ultimate swag.

God is a great salesman. He knows how to recruit people to His cause and sell them on His vision and mission. Yet when God calls out a man, He realizes every one of us has a tattoo across our foreheads that reads: MMFI, or "Make Me Feel Important." Our Father also knows that when He calls out a man, he will have one universal question: WIIFMIIFY, or "What's in It for Me If I Follow You?"

That's why God outlined what lay ahead for Abraham if he accepted this mission impossible. God wanted Abraham to pull up stakes and leave Haran (just north of the Syrian border in Turkey) and trek to Canaan (now modern-day Israel), a formidable journey of four hundred miles. Furthermore, Abraham was seventy-five years old, so he was getting up there in years. Nonetheless, Abraham accepted God's invitation to become the father of a new nation, the first patriarch of His chosen people.

After saying yes to God, Abraham gathered his wife, Sarah,[1] his nephew Lot, everyone in his household, and all his livestock and hit the dusty trail. How Abraham knew where he was going four thousand years ago was a problem that had to have its navigational challenges, but he managed that part well.[2] He built an altar in the new land and dedicated it to the Lord, who, we're told, appeared to Abraham. This happened several times as the nomadic man of God and his clan kept moving south: they'd settle down, build an altar, and worship God.

All good, as they say.

I will now share what happened next through a different lens than this story is traditionally told.

◆   ◆   ◆   ◆

What I'm about to share comes from a unique ethnocentric and ideological perspective. Call it a view of Abraham from the hood, a view from the barrio, a view from the projects of South-Central, or a view from the hollers of West Virginia.

Words like *pimp* and *prostitute* are well-defined concepts and commonly spoken of in the inner city and areas of poverty, where you see pimps driving black Cadillac Escalades with heavy-bass speakers, wearing flamboyant clothes and fur coats in winter, and flashing gold teeth in their mouths and diamond rings on their pinkies.

In the age before the internet, pimps recruited their stables of prostitutes and dropped them off at street corners dressed in high-heeled shoes, short-short leather skirts that hugged their bottoms, and loose tops with plunging necklines. (Now they simply advertise them—wearing even less than that—online.) These women of the night know they have to wear next to nothing to jumpstart the engines of potential customers. They dye their hair all colors of the rainbow and wear gobs of heavy makeup.

What many people don't realize is that pimps often deposit their *wives* or live-in *girlfriends* on street corners or deliver them to hotel lobbies, where they will rendezvous with the john in room 1124—the john who answered the pimp's Craigslist ad. This is done to generate income for the family business...because prostitution in the hood is often a family business.

When a husband pushes his wife into another man's bed for sex and profits financially from the transaction, that's called "pimping." Like the saying goes, if it looks like a duck, waddles like a duck, and quacks like a duck...it's a duck. It certainly ain't no canary. So when I read in Scripture how Abraham treated his wife, Sarah, the roles of pimp and prostitute come readily to my mind.

Here's what happened: after famine struck the land of Canaan, Abraham was forced to gather up his family, his household, and his livestock and travel to Egypt, where there was plenty of food and land for his flocks. This was *another* arduous four-hundred-mile undertaking.

As he approached the border of Egypt, Abraham pulled Sarah aside and said:

Look, you are a very beautiful woman. When the Egyptians see you, they will say, "This is his wife. Let's kill him; then we can have her!" So please tell them you are my sister. Then they will spare my life and treat me well because of their interest in you.
—Genesis 12:11b–13 (NLT)

Since Abraham and Sarah were half-siblings, this message was half-true. But since their primary relationship was as husband and wife, what he told her to say was half-false. But when you get down to the nitty-gritty, this was classic pimp talk. Abraham was looking out for Number 1—himself—so he fed his wife a line of balderdash: "they will spare my life and treat me well…"

He also asked his wife to lie—so he wouldn't have to—when they came upon the Egyptian authorities.

But wait, that's not all!

When this hardy troop settled in Egypt, word of Sarah's great beauty reached the palace officials in Pharaoh's court. They had to check her out because one of the ways they stayed in Pharaoh's good graces was by procuring the hottest-looking women for his harem.

What did a harem look like four thousand years ago? In ancient Egypt, it was a place set aside on palace grounds for the Pharaoh's wives and sexual playthings. The harem could have been its own set of mud-brick buildings surrounded by a high mud-brick wall, or a sectioned-off part of the palace. There was an air of mystery because if any dudes set foot inside the harem without the pharaoh's permission, they swiftly got set up with the potentate's executioner.

Generally speaking, the consorts lived lives of luxury and ease. They had one job and one job only: be readily available to Pharaoh with the understanding that they were to give him mind-blowing sex.

So here's what went down, according to Scripture:

When the palace officials saw her, they sang her praises to
Pharaoh, their king, and Sarai was *taken into his palace.*
Then Pharaoh gave Abram *many gifts* because of her—
sheep, goats, cattle, male and female donkeys, male and
female servants, and camels.
     —Genesis 12:15–16 (NLT) with italics added for
emphasis

Sarah wasn't taken into Pharaoh's palace to play checkers. She had
a job to do, and that was to sexually service him willingly and with
great enthusiasm. She must have thrown herself into the role because
her husband reaped a ton of rewards.

Even though Abraham was paid well for pimping his wife out to
Pharaoh, let's face it: he gave in to fear when he was willing to give up his
wife to preserve his own life, even though God had promised him that he
would become a great nation and that He would make him famous.

Abraham, in the heat of the moment, forgot God's unconditional
promises and caused others great pain and great harm—including
Pharaoh and the Egyptians when God sent terrible plagues upon the
land. After the plagues wreaked havoc in the fields and the populace,
Pharaoh summoned Abraham and demanded to know why he didn't
fess up and say that Sarah was his wife, not his sister.

"Now then, here is your wife," Pharaoh said. "Take her and get
out of here!" (Genesis 12:19b NLT)

Abraham led his family, servants, and livestock back to Canaan,
where the people were "extremely wicked and constantly sinned
against the Lord" (Genesis 13:13 NLT). There he built another altar
to the Lord and worshiped Him. So you would think that Abraham
had learned a valuable lesson and that this is when he went from
pimp to prophet.

Not yet.

When he moved everyone to Gerar in what is today south-central Israel, the local king—a Canaanite named Abimelech—sent for Abraham and Sarah. Call it a social call.

At the king's palace, Abraham introduced his wife, saying, "She is my sister."

Once again, the half-truth was trotted out. Abraham, just like before, was worried that the Canaanite king wouldn't hesitate to kill him if he knew Sarah was his wife and wanted her for his harem. Here's what happened next:

> So King Abimelech of Gerar sent for Sarah and had her brought to him at his palace.
>
> But that night God came to Abimelech in a dream and told him, "You are a dead man, for that woman you have taken is already married!"
>
> But Abimelech had not slept with her yet, so he said, "Lord, will you destroy an innocent nation? Didn't Abraham tell me, 'She is my sister'? And she herself said, 'Yes, he is my brother.' I acted in complete innocence! My hands are clean."
>
> In the dream God responded, "Yes, I know you are innocent. That's why I kept you from sinning against me, and why I did not let you touch her. Now return the woman to her husband, and he will pray for you, for he is a prophet. Then you will live. But if you don't return her to him, you can be sure that you and all your people will die."
>
> Abimelech got up early the next morning and quickly called all his servants together. When he told them what had happened, his men were terrified. Then Abimelech called for Abraham. "What have you done to us?" he demanded. "What crime have I committed that deserves treatment like this, making me and my kingdom guilty of

this great sin? No one should ever do what you have done! Whatever possessed you to do such a thing?"

Abraham replied, "I thought, 'This is a godless place. They will want my wife and will kill me to get her.' And she really is my sister, for we both have the same father, but different mothers. And I married her. When God called me to leave my father's home and to travel from place to place, I told her, 'Do me a favor. Wherever we go, tell the people that I am your brother.'"

Then Abimelech took some of his sheep and goats, cattle, and male and female servants, and he presented them to Abraham. He also returned his wife, Sarah, to him. Then Abimelech said, "Look over my land and choose any place where you would like to live." And he said to Sarah, "Look, I am giving your 'brother' 1,000 pieces of silver in the presence of all these witnesses. This is to compensate you for any wrong I may have done to you. This will settle any claim against me, and your reputation is cleared."

—Genesis 20:2b–16 (NLT)

This section of Scripture would be hilarious if it wasn't so serious. Did you notice how God referred to pimping Abraham? He called him a prophet!

This is the first time in the Bible that the word *prophet* is used— and it refers to a lying pimp. To add insult to injury, God tells Abimelech to let Abraham *pray* for him.

I would imagine that Abimelech wondered to himself, *What kind of religion is this where pimps lie and deceive and wind up as prophets to pray over you?*

When God says He chooses the foolish things of the world to confuse the wise, He wasn't kidding. The lesson here is that no matter how you start off or mess up along the way, God has a plan for your messes, your failures, your setbacks, your shame, and your pain.

Abraham's story is a reminder that it was never too late to be mightily used by God and fulfill his destiny as the father of a great nation and the Lord's prophet.

◆   ◆   ◆   ◆

Abraham's journey is crystalized in the famous story of how God directed this patriarch to take his son Isaac—the one born miraculously from Sarah after a lifetime of infertility—to the land of Moriah and sacrifice him on a mountain.

This is one of my favorite stories in the Bible. Think about it: Abraham had been waiting for his promised son for twenty-five years. A miracle child is born from a woman whose womb was barren. Sarah is so astonished to give birth that she calls him Isaac, which means *make me laugh.*

And now Abraham hears God calling him to offer Isaac as a burnt sacrifice. After three days of traveling with several servants, they arrive at the foot of the mountain. "Stay here," Abraham tells his servants. "The boy and I will go worship, and then we will return to you."

We will return to you.

Did you catch that? Abraham was saying to his servants, in so many words, *I trust in my God. I believe in my God. I live by the word of my God. I know Him, and He cannot lie. Even though He may slay me, I will trust in Him.*

To fully understand the amazing faith that Abraham now had, we must first understand how horrific and awful a burnt sacrifice actually was in those days. Here are the steps:

1. Cut the throat of the animal so it can bleed to death
2. Skin the animal completely and burn the skin on the fire
3. Gut the animal and place the innards on the fire

4. Chop up the remaining parts of the sacrifice and place
   them on the fire

This is what Abraham was being asked by God to do *to his own son*. Yet he obeyed, which is why Abraham is called a "friend of God" several times in Scripture, most notably in James 2:23 (NIV), which says, "he was called God's friend."

Why did God want a friend?

God knew a day would come when He would sacrifice His own Son in a horrific way and watch Him suffer in agony. He knew He would be forced to turn His back on His dying Son. He knew He would hear His Son scream out, "My God, My God, why have You forsaken Me?" (Matthew 27:46b NKJV)

At the moment, God wanted a friend to understand His pain as a father. Abraham was that friend He could turn to for understanding.

So what's the lesson for us?

Jesus talked about men who will be His true disciples. He said, "Whoever wants to be my disciple must deny themselves and take up their cross and follow me" (Matthew 16:24 NIV).

When God calls you to His service, He will ask you if you can give everything up and put it on the altar of sacrifice as a sign of faith and obedience. He does that so you can have it all.

God has called you to serve Him, but perhaps there is something you can't seem to let go of, and it's holding you back. You can't go to the next level with Him until you can let this thing go.

◆   ◆   ◆   ◆

I understand this concept well because I went through something similar to Abraham's experience on Moriah.

When I was growing up in the church, I was not a praise person or a worshiper. Pastor Hawkins, who was a Marine, taught by example, and that example was that men in the Baptist church should be stoic, unemotional, and austere.

I can remember watching him sit in his chair next to the pulpit and not crack a smile or show too much emotion during our praise-and-worship time. Sure, it was fine that the women shouted and danced in joy before the Lord, but the men needed to hold back and not be swept up in the emotion of the moment. We were to be scholars of the Bible, men of honor: tough, hard, and proud.

Consequently, I learned to be stoic and austere as well. I wasn't one of the praise people and wouldn't get emotionally involved when the choir would sing at the top of their lungs and the women would dance in the pews. In other words, I learned to be a man of stone.

As I developed into an adult and became a father, I found myself to still be somewhat spiritually cold, austere, and aloof. This continued into my twenties, even more so when I became successful beyond all my dreams. I was receiving huge bonus checks at work, receiving praise and royalties following the release of my first book (a business book called *On Teams*), and supervising the construction of my dream home. I was so full of myself that it's no wonder I came across as arrogant. After all, I was achieving dreams that I never thought possible.

At the time, I was coaching a Pop Warner football team called the Strongsville Archers. We became the most feared team in the league. After our team had won many championships, my son, Chris, turned ten, meaning he was finally old enough to play.

He was tremendously excited to get on the team. I remember dressing Chris on his first game day, helping him put on his jersey and pads. "Dad, make me a beast," he said.

"I will," I joshed back, patting him on the head.

Our friends and family members came from all around to see my son play his first game. As he ran onto the field, he looked back at me and said, "Dad, I love you."

"Love you too, son," I replied.

On the very first play of his very first game, Chris took a terrific hit, breaking his neck, which paralyzed him. He fell to the ground like a rag doll. I knew he was severely injured.

I sprinted onto the field. The first thing I saw, through the earholes of his helmet, was that he was bleeding from his ears. He looked up to me and said, "Dad, where's my body? I can't feel my body."

I had never felt so helpless. Shock and disbelief ran through my body as I saw my ten-year-old son lying on the ground, paralyzed from the big hit he had taken. Thanks be to God there was a paramedic in the stands (whose last name, incidentally, was also Archer). He called for an ambulance and helped the EMTs put my son in the van. I hopped in as well for the drive to the hospital.

After stabilizing him, the doctors took a saw and cut my son's football helmet off. Chris was petrified by the sound of the saw whizzing over his head. All I could do was watch from the side, again feeling helpless.

Once the helmet was off, he was dashed to the tomography room where they did a CT scan. Along the way, one of the doctors pulled me aside and said, "You might want to prepare yourself for having a son who is a quadriplegic."

Shivers went down my spine.

After the scan, doctors put a circular metal-framed halo on Chris's head, secured by four bolts into the skull, to keep him immobile. As I sat at his bedside, I couldn't help but think I was in a hospital room with a paralyzed son. All the money I had earned, all the fame I had acquired, all the copies of my book that I had sold, all the furniture filling the big house I had built, and all my work as a chaplain for the Cleveland Browns—none of those things could help me.

I'll never forget when one of the rival Pop Warner coaches who didn't like my arrogance stuck his head in our room and said, "Hey, big shot, where is your God now?"

What a cruel thing to say, but I will admit that I was thinking the same exact thing.

Everyone knew I was a man of God. Everyone knew I was a man of prayer. I looked up to Heaven and said, "God, I must have coached a thousand kids over the years, and no one has ever been severely injured. Why would You do this to me and my son?"

That night, the hospital room was dark. I heard various instruments beeping. Other than that, it was deathly quiet.

Then I heard a Voice speak to me. It said, "Praise Me now."

I shook my head. I thought I was losing my mind, perhaps from the stress of dealing with a paralyzed son who would be restricted to a wheelchair for the rest of his life.

A thought came to mind: *I don't praise God in church, so why would I praise Him in the hospital with my son being paralyzed?*

And the Voice spoke again. "Praise Me now," He said.

I knew it was the Lord speaking to my heart. So I obeyed. I began to praise God quietly in my own mind, which was an incredibly difficult thing to do in that moment. I was in pain and sorrow and confusion, but the Voice kept saying, "Praise Me now."

At first, I just began to repeat Scriptures that I had memorized over the years. Verses such as Psalm 34:1 (KJV): "I will bless the Lord at all times; his praise shall continually be in my mouth."

Next was Psalm 118:24 (KJV): "This is the day which the Lord hath made; let us rejoice and be glad in it."

Next was Psalm 27:1 (KJV): "The Lord is my light and my salvation; whom shall I fear? The Lord is the strength of my life; of whom shall I be afraid?"

Next, I began to thank God for all that He had done for me and my family. I thanked God for the salvation of my mom, my sister, and my aunts. I thanked God for the abundant provision He had bestowed upon me, the selling of the book, and the house He provided. I thanked God for His Son's dying on the cross for me and all His mercy and grace in my life.

Then I began to repent of my arrogance, my self-centeredness, and my trust in my ability and strength, and I told Him how wrong I was. I repented for how aloof I had been to others and how I was unwilling to praise Him and worship Him because I thought I was so cool.

I began to cry and weep, and before I knew it, I was on the floor of the hospital room where my son was lying in a bed, paralyzed and sleeping. With my face on the ground, I wept and asked God for mercy and grace and not to judge my son because of my sin.

One of the things that frightened me was that in the Bible, whenever God wanted to truly get a man's attention, He would not judge the man, but He would judge the man's son.

When Pharaoh refused to let the Hebrews go after four hundred years of slavery in Egypt, it was his firstborn son who died. When David had an affair with Bathsheba, it was their newborn son who perished.

I was so afraid that my proud, haughty mindset had caused God to judge my son. I wept and wailed, "Lord, please have mercy on my son. Do not judge him because of what I've done. He's only ten years old, Lord, with his whole life ahead of him." My pleas came from deep within me.

I did this for three days, praising and worshiping God in the hospital room.

One afternoon, I needed to go to the restroom. I'm sure I looked terrible, since I hadn't left my paralyzed son in three days. My clothes were wrinkled and a stubbly beard was growing on my face.

As I moved past the foot of Chris's bed, I flicked his big toe— something I used to do when I put him to bed growing up.

"Ouch," he said.

What?

I touched his big toe again. "You can feel that?"

"Yes, Dad."

I ran to the nurses' station. "We need to get a doctor in here right away! My son has feeling in his toes!"

Two doctors hustled in. They confirmed that Chris had feeling in his toes, his legs, and his arms.

"This is a miracle," one said.

A few days later, Chris left the hospital under his own power, fully restored to good health. I count this as the greatest miracle of my life.

From that moment on, whatever God needed me to do for Him, I did. My son and I have since preached together in Germany, in the Dominican Republic, and in Florida. We have worked together for the Lord.

Chris got a tattoo on his arm that says *I can do all things through Christ who gives me strength* from Philippians 4:13. He joined the military and became a great soldier for the Lord and for his country. Every time I see him, I thank God for His mercy and grace, but I also know that I understand the story of Abraham and how he became ready to sacrifice his son a lot better.

What I've learned is that one of the most important things God wants from His men is a broken and contrite heart, which He will not despise (Psalm 51:17). It's amazing what God can do through brokenness and humility. When my son went down on the football field that day, I was completely broken and shattered, but God used that to change me.

Great things come from brokenness, and great things can come from the power of one man who humbles himself before Almighty God.

◆   ◆   ◆   ◆

Discussion Questions

1. Is there a generational stronghold that you might have in your family? If so, what is it?
2. Have you decided that this generational stronghold will end with you? What steps will you take to make that happen?

3. What situations make you afraid enough to be a coward?
4. Abraham really mistreated Sarah. How do you treat women? How do you view women?
5. Even when Abraham was not acting like a prophet, God called him one. Have you forgiven yourself for your failures? What failures haunt you to the point that you just can't let go?

6

One Man's Story: David, from Illegitimate Son to Anointed King

I'm going to do something a bit different with this chapter: I'm going to tell you some little-known information about David and the cast of characters around him. The following will be a bit more Bible exploration than I normally do in a book, but you'll see why if you hang with me.

If you read *What Belief Can Do,* then you're well aware that not only was I not raised in a Christian home, but I didn't have a legacy from my family's past to build upon.

My guess is that 50 percent of the men holding this book also don't have a godly legacy they can bank on. If that's the case for you, I want to give you hope that not only can you start your own legacy today, but God will help you do it.

So stick with me as I talk about David and just how high the odds were stacked against him.

◆   ◆   ◆   ◆

Whenever a huge underdog team walks onto the gridiron, the baseball field, or a sheet of ice, sportswriters looking for a quick metaphor will frame the contest as a "David versus Goliath" match.

They spin this narrative to show in very few words that a plucky, undermanned, but brainy team will have to strategically outwit and outplay its opponent if it hopes to win. This, of course, is based on the story of how a shepherd boy named David annihilated a cocky nine-foot-tall giant named Goliath, which has been part of our cultural consciousness for three thousand years.

David certainly wasn't the betting favorite when he entered the arena to take on Goliath. The sports books in Las Vegas would have taken this match off the boards. David would have been deemed to have no chance of surviving a one-on-one encounter with a warrior far taller, stronger, and better equipped than he was.

Instead, David flipped the script with a flick of his wrist. When he took out Goliath, David became Israel's champion—and we're still talking about what he did with his slingshot thousands of years later.

There are a couple of points I want to make about David that you probably haven't heard. The first involves a dark secret that few people are aware of. It's not that David tried to keep this information a secret, but many of us never looked deeply enough to connect the dots.

Let's back up and look at David's story from the beginning. In 1 Samuel, we learn that the high priest Eli (who was also a judge) had a close relationship with God and understood His purpose for his life. Eli's sons, however, were a different story. They defrauded people, were sacrilegious, and allowed the Ark of the Covenant to fall into enemy hands. In addition, the nation of Israel fell completely away from God on their watch. When Eli died, Israel entered a new era in which the influence of the priests declined and that of the prophets grew.

Samuel was the first of these prophets and was committed to leading the nation back to right living. Since the Israelites continued to suffer from corrupt priests and judges, they yearned to be ruled by a king. The people thought that having a king would make their lives better and put them on par with the surrounding nations.

After the people demanded a king, God directed Samuel to anoint Saul, a tall, good-looking man from the tribe of Benjamin, as the nation's first. Saul's early reign was marked by leadership and bravery, but then the wheels started coming off. Over time, he proved to be arrogant and rebellious. Serving the Lord was not Saul's first priority; maintaining power was.

Because God was displeased, He commissioned Samuel to anoint one of the sons of Jesse of Bethlehem as the next king, someone whose heart was connected to Him. With great fanfare, Samuel approached the elders of Bethlehem for an important meeting; the elders thought they were in big trouble. After all, everyone knew that Samuel was a mighty man of God and a big-time prophet. The elders worried that Samuel had come to their village with a dire prophecy of doom in his hip pocket.

Instead, Samuel asked to see Jesse and his sons. Here's how 1 Samuel 16:7, 10–12 (NLT) describes what happened next:

> But the Lord said to Samuel, "Don't judge by his appearance or height, for I have rejected him. The Lord doesn't see things the way you see them. People judge by outward appearance, but the Lord looks at the heart."
>
> In the same way all seven of Jesse's sons were presented to Samuel. But Samuel said to Jesse, "The Lord has not chosen any of these." Then Samuel asked, "Are these all the sons you have?"
>
> "There is still the youngest," Jesse replied. "But he's out in the fields watching the sheep and goats."

"Send for him at once," Samuel said. "We will not sit down to eat until he arrives."

So Jesse sent for him. He was dark and handsome, with beautiful eyes.

And the Lord said, "This is the one; anoint him."

That's exactly what Samuel did. He took a flask of olive oil and anointed David. "And the Spirit of the LORD came powerfully upon David from that day on," Scripture says in 1 Samuel 16:13.

I've always been curious why David was not included in the initial roll call of sons. Traditional biblical scholars believe David was omitted because he was the youngest one, as if that were a black mark against him. But I don't believe this theory holds up under closer scrutiny of the account relayed here in Scripture.

When Samuel arrived in Bethlehem and approached the town elders, the Bible tells us they were "trembling to meet him" (verse 4), meaning they were terrified of the prophet. If Samuel asked them to jump, their response would be "How high?"

So when Samuel requested a special meeting with Jesse and his sons, all were expected to show up. This means there must have been some convincing reason for Jesse *not* to extend an invitation to David.

So why was he excluded?

I believe David provides the answer to this question in Psalm 51, which he penned in the chaotic aftermath of his adulterous affair with Bathsheba.

He wrote:

> Behold, I was brought forth in iniquity,
> And in sin my mother conceived me.
> —Psalm 51:5 (NKJV)

So what is David trying to tell us in this verse?

Most believe David was explaining that his affair with Bathsheba was due to the sin nature that plagues all mankind because of Adam and Eve's original sin. This does not explain *why* David committed adultery, however. (Though all humans have the same sin nature, not all commit adultery.)

Setting aside all fancy theological interpretations, I'm interpreting verse 5 simply as it reads: "in sin my mother conceived me" means exactly what it says—David's mother conceived him in an act of sin. She must have committed adultery, and David was the byproduct of this infidelity.

This would explain why David was not initially included in the meeting with Samuel: technically, it could be argued that David was not a true son of Jesse, but only a half-brother to the other seven. However, God did include David as part of Jesse's family, much in the same way Jesus was considered a son of Joseph even though He was conceived by the Holy Spirit.

Which leads to the next question: Who was David's mother?

This is where things get interesting. Nowhere in Scripture is David's mother mentioned by name. This is noteworthy and a bit unusual because the mothers of several ancient prophets and patriarchs are not only mentioned but described as playing significant roles in the upbringing of their children, such as Moses's mother Jochebed (Exodus 6:20) and Samuel's mother Hannah (1 Samuel 1:1–20). David's mother, if she committed adultery, brought shame upon Jesse and his family. It's not surprising her name was excised from the biblical account.

Then again, it's entirely possible that Jesse was the unfaithful one. Perhaps he had an affair with another woman, married or unmarried, who gave birth to David.

A third theory to consider is that David's mother was a prostitute. Back then, it wasn't uncommon for children born from an illicit relationship to live with the father. In the Book of Judges, which predates

David's time, there's a story about Jephthah, who was conceived when his father Gilead had sexual relations with a prostitute:

> Jephthah the Gileadite was a mighty warrior. His father was Gilead; his mother was a prostitute. Gilead's wife also bore him sons, and when they were grown up, they drove Jephthah away. "You are not going to get any inheritance in our family," they said, "because you are the son of another woman."
> —Judges 11:1–2 (NIV)

Though conceived through this illicit encounter, Jephthah nevertheless grew up in Gilead's house, where the father took responsibility for raising the child.

As Jephthah grew older, this created a tremendous tension with the sons born of the true mother. They eventually drove Jephthah out of the family to prevent him from receiving any of his father's inheritance.

If David's mother was a prostitute, it would explain why she isn't mentioned. I also suspect that his brothers pushed their father not to include David when Samuel called for a meeting with the sons of Jesse.

There's one more clue to consider.

David referred to his mother one other time, in Psalm 69, a psalm which—next to Psalm 23—is the most quoted in the New Testament. It's generally believed Psalm 69 covers David's early life prior to his anointing by Samuel as well as a prophetic vision about Christ. I want to focus on the historical aspect of the psalm and not the prophetic side.

In Psalm 69:8 (NASB), David wrote this:

> I have become estranged from my brothers
> And an alien to my mother's sons.

It's fascinating to me to see how David seems to be talking about two groups of children. It's clear that he was estranged from his brothers (Jesse's family) *and* an alien to his mother's children, which implies that both sets of children rejected David. This supports the idea that his mother was either a prostitute (with other children) or possibly another married woman whose husband rejected David, forcing Jesse to look after his illegitimate son.

No wonder things got sticky when Samuel rolled into town and asked to meet with the sons of Jesse.

According to *Strong's Dictionary of the Bible*, the Hebrew word for estranged, *zur*, means to "turn one aside from lodging" and can also refer to a person who has come from "adultery—to come from another man" or another woman. In fact, the word is rooted in the Hebrew word *mamzer*, which means "bastard or illegitimate." *Zur* implies David was not included in regular family activities such as mealtimes.

One thing oddly missing in Psalm 69 is any mention of David's relationship with Jesse. Not once did David point to his father as the source of his misery. Neither do we see any hint of conflict when Jesse asked David to take food to his brothers who were fighting the Philistines—but as soon as David shows up at the army camp, one reads about the animosity between him and his half-brothers (1 Samuel 17:28–29).

Psalm 69 also addresses the misery David endured growing up. Because of his mother's sin, David's childhood was full of loneliness and rejection. He speaks of hours spent crying because of the rejection (verse 3). He explains his frustration at being punished for a sin he did not commit (verse 4)—his mother's sin. Worse, he became the object of mockery as drunkards sang about his plight (verse 12).

David's life also became a byword or proverb—literally a living warning—of what happens to those whose mothers commit adultery:

When I made sackcloth my clothing,
I became a byword to them.
Those who sit in the gate talk about me....
    —Psalm 69:11–12a (NASB)

What was particularly hurtful was that those who "sit in the gate" used him as an example (verse 12) of what happens when people sin. The term "sit in the gate" refers to the elders of the city, who sat at the main entrance into the town or city and made judgments on cases (see Proverbs 31:23 and Deuteronomy 21:19; 22:15). These would be the same elders of Bethlehem who didn't think it necessary for Jesse to include David when Samuel wanted to meet Jesse's sons.

David then adds his thoughts about carrying the personal shame of his mother's sin:

You know my reproach and my shame and my dishonor;
All my adversaries are before You.
Reproach has broken my heart and I am so sick.
And I looked for sympathy, but there was none,
And for comforters, but I found none.
    —Psalm 69:19–20 (NASB)

No one cared that David was the innocent byproduct of his mother's sin. Furthermore, the Jews believed that children could be punished for the sins of the parents. We see a hint of this in the gospels, when the disciples—after stumbling upon a blind man—asked Jesus if he was being punished for the sins of his parents or for his own sin (John 9:2–3).

Though David was despised and rejected by his family, humiliated by those in his hometown, and given a lowly job of tending the sheep, God knew his heart and how he responded to the rejection and ugliness that filled his childhood. This is why He chose this boy as the next king of Israel, which gives us a keen insight into God's redemptive nature. It's clear that the Lord will use anyone in spite of his or her background and heritage as long as he or she has a heart for Him.

◆   ◆   ◆   ◆

This chapter would not be complete without giving a nod to the power of one man to change the tide of history and do mighty things on behalf of God's Kingdom. David's courageous confrontation with Goliath helped him overcome his bastard status and set the stage for him to eventually become the king of Israel, as well as the author of psalms that still resonate in our hearts thousands of years later.

There are a few more things I want to say about this incredible warrior, so hang with me as we go back to the beginning, when Samuel anointed Saul as Israel's first king and Saul was given one assignment by God: to destroy the Amalekites.

God said, "OK, Saul, now that you're king, I want you to wipe out the nation that abused and afflicted the people of Israel when they were coming out of bondage in Egypt. I gave Moses My word that I would destroy the Amalekites one day and avenge the nation of Israel."

What God was saying to Saul was this: *Make good on My promise to Moses. I am the Lord God, so I cannot lie. I'm leaving it to you to fulfill what I said I would do for My chosen people.*

When God instructed Saul to wipe out the Amalekites, He meant that all men, women, and children, as well as their sheep, cattle, goats, and livestock, were to be killed—destroyed completely.

When the Israelite army arrived in the land of the Amalekites, however, they discovered an opulent place of wealth and prosperity.

The sheep were so fat that they had to roll on the ground. The cows were content and plentiful. This was the land of milk and honey.

The soldiers said to Saul, "Are you sure God wants us to do this—wipe all this out? We should take these riches back home with us."

So Saul and his army destroyed the Amalekites—but only up to a point. Saul didn't kill the Amalekite king. He didn't slaughter every animal that was there. Instead, he and his men returned to Israel with King Agag and the best of the sheep, goats, cattle, and plunder. In other words, Saul did God's will his way, which was halfway.

Back on home soil, surrounded by his victorious army, Saul was putting on a big barbecue to celebrate the victory when the prophet Samuel suddenly showed up.

"Did you do what God called you to do?" Samuel asked the king.

"Of course I did," Saul replied.

"Then what is that bleating of the sheep I hear in my ears?"

Samuel had him there.

Saul justified his halfway measures because he wanted to be a people-pleaser. By giving in to their requests for the finest sheep, goats, and cattle, Saul proved that he was a people-pleaser, not a God-pleaser.

In response, Samuel basically said this to Saul: "You have disobeyed the Lord God. On this most important thing, you made God out to be a liar. You did not do what He promised Moses that He would do. As a punishment, the Spirit of God will be removed from you. Your anointing will be gone."

Saul was crestfallen—and panic-stricken. He grabbed Samuel's cloak, tearing it. Samuel turned and looked at him. "The same way you've torn this piece of cloth from my robe, God is going to tear the kingdom out of your hand," the prophet said. "He's going to find another man to replace you, a man after His own heart."

That man—a young man—was David, who was anointed by Samuel in secret.

As it happens, Saul was afflicted with a tormenting spirit. The only thing that could soothe his jittery nerves was music. Someone told Saul there was a shepherd kid who was talented with the harp, so David was brought to the palace to play for the king. This also allowed David—the future king that no one knew about—to see how palace life functioned.

At the time, war clouds were forming. A neighboring nation and hated enemy, the Philistines, mustered their army for battle. Saul gathered his troops. The two armies camped on opposite sides of the Valley of Elah, marking time because whoever rushed down the valley and up the steep cliffs to attack would be at a disadvantage. The waiting game resulted in a forty-day stalemate.

Ratcheting up the tension was the daily appearance of a Philistine soldier named Goliath, who marched out and taunted the Israelites for being a bunch of wussies.

Goliath is described as being over nine feet tall at a time when the average male height was much shorter than it is today, so he was *really* tall. He wore a bronze helmet and a bronze coat of mail that weighed 125 pounds. Goliath strapped bronze armor on his legs and carried a bronze javelin on his shoulder.

Because of his unique height and muscular build that resembled a WWE wrestler, Goliath was trained for one thing and one thing only: to intimidate the enemy and kill them. Brute force reigned in the ancient world, so when David saw how Goliath was taunting God's chosen people, he said he'd take on the giant, knowing there was just one rule for their *mano a mano* battle: there were no rules.

By the time David approached Goliath in the middle of the valley, surrounded by soldiers from both armies, the shepherd boy had a game plan: use his sling to fling a flat, smooth rock at Goliath's head. Malcolm Gladwell, author of *David and Goliath: Underdogs, Misfits, and the Art of Battling Giants*, wrote that a sling could be an incredibly devastating weapon. There were no ballistics checks in those days, but the stopping power of a rock fired from David's sling was roughly equal to the stopping power of a .45-caliber handgun.

David reared back, spun the slingshot around his head, and delivered his pitch. We know David's aim was true, and down went Goliath. David grabbed the giant's sword and cut his head off. The rest of Israel's army attacked and routed the Philistines.

Saul had promised a huge reward to anyone who killed Goliath, including one of his daughters in marriage and tax-free status for the victor's entire family. At first, Saul loved David, and the feeling was mutual—but that all changed when Saul and David returned to the palace and the women sang out: *Saul has killed his thousands and David his tens of thousands,* which sure sounded like a put-down to Saul's ears. From that point on, Saul viewed David as a threat because he knew God was with him.

Sometimes a man can be a lid and not a leader. A lid is insecure. A lid is easily threatened. A lid can be removed. A lid has his own agenda. A lid wants to repress people. Saul was a lid, much in the way Henry Ford II was a lid back in the 1960s.

Back in 1964, the Ford Mustang was unveiled at the New York World's Fair by Lee Iacocca, head of the Ford Division. When the Mustang became a huge hit, it was Iacocca who landed on the covers of *Time* and *Newsweek* magazines. It was Iacocca who was the subject of laudatory profiles on television and in newspapers. It was Iacocca who received much praise and adoration from people everywhere he traveled. Henry Ford II became so jealous of Iacocca's ascension that he had him fired. That's the definition of a leader who's a lid.

Saul was similarly jealous of David and his newfound popularity. *How can this upstart steal my thunder? Doesn't David realize I'm the king of Israel?*

Unlike Henry Ford II, Saul didn't have the option of firing David. If Saul wanted him gone, that meant he had to be killed. That's how kings rolled in those days.

Saul was also looking out for his legacy. Even though he was Israel's first king, he assumed that his reign was the start of a family dynasty. His son Jonathan was the crown prince, which meant that one day he'd wear his crown.

But Jonathan was at the Valley of Elah when David killed Goliath, and he was amazed by the power and the courage of this young man. Jonathan was also spiritually mature enough to realize that the hand of the Almighty God was on David, not on him.

Despite being passed over, he and David became best friends—like they were close brothers. While his father was insanely jealous, Jonathan didn't feel threatened by David. He even took steps to protect David and school him on palace life.

You see, David was basically a country boy. He had grass in his teeth since he came from the sheep fields surrounding the small town called Bethlehem. When David started hanging around Saul's palace, he needed to be coached and nurtured. He needed polish.

"I know the hand of God is on you, and you're going to be king," Jonathan said. "When that happens, all I ask is that you extend the same love, mercy, and grace that I'm giving you now to my family."

That day, Jonathan made a covenant, or solemn pact, with David by taking off his robe and giving it to David, together with his tunic, sword, bow, and belt (1 Samuel 18:3). For David's side, I believe they followed the custom of the day when each of them made a cut in their arms and matched the blood together. Now they each had a scar to remind them of their "blood covenant."

Later on, Jonathan helped David escape his father's clutches and flee to Judah, the southern portion of Israel. As an outlaw with a price on his head, David was like a Robin Hood, protecting the local people from bandits and righting wrongs.

Several years later, the Philistines were back on the warpath. In another huge battle, Saul was hit by several arrows from enemy archers, and Jonathan was killed in the heat of the battle.

The severely wounded king ordered his armor bearer to kill him so that he wouldn't fall into the Philistines' hands and be tortured. When the armor bearer couldn't bring himself to follow through, Saul took his sword and fell on it, committing suicide.

Following the massive defeat, the nation of Israel split into two: David became king of Judah, and Saul's son, Ishbosheth, became king of Israel. A civil war ensued, which ended with the murder of Ishbosheth by his own courtiers and the anointing of David as king over all Israel.

One day after consolidating power, David asked: "Is anyone in Saul's family still alive—anyone to whom I can show kindness for Jonathan's sake?" (2 Samuel 9:1 NLT)

That was an extraordinary request because when a new king came into power, one of his first assignments was to kill anybody left over from the old regime.

There's precedence for this in the lion kingdom. When a lion takes over a pride, his first job is to kill all the cubs so that he can then produce his own. Similarly, the first job of a monarch, after coming into power, was to search for anyone left from the old kingdom and have them executed because they could make a claim to the throne based upon the royal blood flowing through their veins.

One of Saul's servants, Ziba, said Saul had a grandson named Mephibosheth, who happened to be Jonathan's son. What follows is a sad story.

Mephibosheth was five years old, being looked after by a nurse, when Saul and Jonathan were killed on the battlefield. The nurse was fully aware that the Philistines would kill this youngster because he was in line to be king.

Consider This...

Every character in the story of David and Mephibosheth represents somebody in the Gospel narrative:

- David represents God the Father. He is the king: judge, jury, and executioner.
- Saul represents Adam, a rebellious, I'll-do-it-my-way individual who cripples all humanity.
- Mephibosheth represents humanity because his grandfather's rebellion against God caused him to go from the palace to the pit.
- Jonathan represents Jesus. He is the son of the king with mercy and grace who created a blood covenant with David.
- Ziba represents the Holy Spirit, who was sent by the king to fetch the crippled son and bring him back to the palace for restoration.

That's what the Holy Spirit does in our lives: He finds us, He grabs us, He pulls us, and He carries us into the presence of Almighty God. And that's how God wants to use your story. He wants you to somehow—and in some way—show others the glory of Christ when you show mercy and grace.

I don't care what kind of generational curses may exist in your family—alcoholism, gambling, drug abuse, being unfaithful to women—whatever's in your family lineage. No matter what your dad, granddad, or great-granddad did to bring shame and ill repute to your family, you can be the one who says, "It stops here. It stops today. It stops with me."

You have the power as one man to stand against history and say, "I will be different."

David made that choice to be different, and so can you.

In fear, she ran with the boy in her arms, but tripped and dropped him—likely from some sort of balcony. The boy fell to the ground with a thud. Although he survived, Mephibosheth's legs were broken. His feet were warped. He was crippled for life.

With great anxiety, the nurse picked him up and fled to a place on the east side of the Jordan River called Lo-debar, which in Hebrew means "a place of no pasture," a place of no hope. We would call that being on the wrong side of the tracks, meaning that Mephibosheth went to the ghetto. He went to the hood. He went to poverty. He had been taken to a place that wasn't flowing with milk and honey.

And then the new king of Israel called for him. When Mephibosheth, now an adult, was brought into David's presence, the king told him, "I didn't bring you here to execute you, even though that is my right. I intend to show kindness to you because of my promise to your father, Jonathan. I will give you all the property that once belonged to your grandfather Saul, and you will eat with me at the king's table."

Mephibosheth bowed respectfully. "Why are you showing such kindness to a dead dog like me?" he asked.

Let's stop here for a moment. If you called yourself a dog in those days, that was about as low as you could go because dogs were not viewed as "man's best friend" or household pets like they are today.

Dogs were scavengers. They were mangy. They ran in wild packs. They attacked your livestock. They attacked small babies. They had diseases. They were like gigantic rats, so to call yourself a dog was to do yourself a tremendous disservice. It meant you were at the bottom of the heap.

But Mephibosheth took that a step further by calling himself a "dead dog," which meant he had no hope, no future—nothing. Yet David told Mephibosheth that not only would he show him kindness, but he could hang out with him during the nightly banquets.

Here's the lesson we can all benefit from: You, as one man, can change the trajectory of your family based upon your obedience or disobedience to God. Throughout Scripture, we can see the consequences of not obeying God. It happened to Adam and Eve: when they disobeyed, they were banished from the Garden of Eden. It happened to Cain: when he disobeyed God's directive to offer a firstborn from his flock and offered fruit instead, he felt compelled to murder Abel, whose sacrifice was well-received by the Lord. It happened to Pharaoh: when he disobeyed, his firstborn was killed. And it happened to Saul when he failed to wipe out the Amalekites completely.

The upshot: One man, depending upon whether he obeys or disobeys God, can impact himself, his family, and those around him for years and years.

The lesson here is that every man can choose his sin. We are free-willed creatures who can get caught up in drug use, gambling, adultery, and stealing. While we are free to choose our sins, we cannot choose the *consequences* of those sins or how long those consequences are going to last.

That's why I like to tell men that if you're not going to be obedient for yourself, then be obedient for the generations to follow. King David, who understood what it was like to be illegitimate and forsaken, to be rejected by both his father and his mentor Saul, used that understanding to turn his pain into power, his wounds into wisdom, and his tragedy into triumph. His life became a demonstration of mercy and grace.

That's the power of one man.

Here's the final lesson to remember: *Man's rejected is God's selected.* The Bible says Jesus came to His own, and His own received Him not. He was rejected by men, but He was selected by God.

If you've been rejected, if you've been set aside, if you've been mistreated, if you've been thrown to the curb, you are ready for your promotion because God uses greatly those who have been wounded very deeply.

That's the power of one man, and that's the power of David, who went from illegitimate son to the anointed king of Israel.

◆   ◆   ◆   ◆

Discussion Questions

1. When and where were you rejected, and how did it affect you?
2. We know that Mephibosheth became crippled because he was dropped by somebody he trusted. Who dropped you? And how has it affected you as a man today?
3. God has extended mercy and grace to you. Who can you extend mercy and grace to?
4. What relationships would you like to restore that are broken?
5. What generational curses in your family have flowed for two or three generations? Can you say no to domestic abuse, to alcoholism, to pornography addiction, to drug addiction, to having a cold, distant personality, or to having kids out of wedlock?

7

One Man's Story: The Apostle Paul and His Road to Transformation

M y last example of the power of one man comes from the Apostle Paul, who had quite the résumé.

Author of thirteen letters or epistles in the New Testament.[1]

Influential teacher conversant in Aramaic, Hebrew, Greek, and Latin, the preeminent language of imperial administration, legislation, and the military at the time of Christ.

Missionary to much of Asia Minor and present-day Greece.

The most incredible apologist of the Gospel and how to live a Christian life.

Nearly two thousand years later, we can tell how deep a thinker Paul was by reading his books in the Bible. Even translations into modern English like the New Living Translation or The Message show that he was no intellectual lightweight.

Compared to the other men of God that I've talked about so far, we have a greater picture of Paul's background, thanks to Luke, who wrote about Paul in the Book of Acts, and from little asides that Paul shared in his numerous letters.

For instance, Paul was named Saul when he was born in the city of Tarsus in the region of Cilicia. Tarsus is still around today, located in the modern-day province of Mersin, Turkey, twelve miles inland from the Mediterranean coast and surrounded by fertile plains. The Cydnus River connects the city with the Mediterranean Sea.

This area of Turkey is one of the oldest continually inhabited urban centers in the world, dating back six thousand years. A bit of trivia: according to Plutarch, Cleopatra met Mark Antony aboard her ship outside the city's port-side gate. Alexander the Great recuperated in Tarsus after falling ill there while swimming in the river.

Before Paul's time, various conquerors batted Tarsus like a piñata. The vibrant city changed hands numerous times because of its importance as a trade port. At different times, the Hittites, the Assyrians, and the Persians controlled the region—and thus its key role in commerce. When Saul was born in 5 AD to Jewish parents, Tarsus was firmly in the hands of the Romans.

Sometime during his childhood, Saul's family moved to Jerusalem, where his father became a member of the Pharisees, comprised of middle-class businessmen and local leaders of the synagogues. Saul's father derived his income from leather goods and tentmaking, so the family had the means necessary to let Saul study under the famous teacher Gamaliel.

Pharisees were known for their holier-than-thou personal piety, for teaching that Jews should observe hundreds and hundreds of laws in the Torah, and their acceptance of oral tradition.

In fact, the Pharisees embraced the idea that oral tradition—dating all the way back to Moses—deserved equal authority with the written Word of God. There's just one small problem with that: "oral tradition" carries as much legal weight as, say, an oral promise to purchase a home. In a sense, oral tradition had the effect of *adding* to God's Word and making it say whatever you wanted it to.

This explains why Jesus called out the Pharisees on numerous occasions, including the time He quoted the prophet Isaiah:

> These people honor me with their lips,
> but their hearts are far from me.
> Their worship is a farce,
> for they teach man-made ideas as commands from God.
>   —Mark 7:6b–7 (NLT)

Yet Saul was all in, calling himself a "real Hebrew if there ever was one! I was a member of the Pharisees, who demand the strictest obedience to the Jewish law" (Philippians 3:5b NLT).

Saul would have been in his mid-twenties when Jesus was crucified in Jerusalem. Although there's no mention of Saul participating in the machinations that produced the death sentence for Jesus, one can be awfully certain he knew what was going on. We do know that shortly after the Resurrection, he grabbed the reins of leadership and wreaked havoc on the Church, making house-to-house searches for Christ-followers and dragging both men and women into prison.

When Stephen, one of Jesus's followers, failed to recant his testimony before the High Council, the Jewish leaders were practically frothing at the mouth to kill the man. Scripture tells us they rushed Stephen and dragged him out of the city to stone him to death. Before they threw their first rock, though, they handed their coats to Saul for safekeeping—so he was an eyewitness to (as well as complicit in) this horrible murder.

And then many of us know about the "road to Damascus" story, one of the most dramatic moments in the Bible. Saul, with a letter from the High Council in his pouch giving him permission to round up Christians in Damascus and bring them back to Jerusalem in chains, took a posse with him. As the crow flies, Damascus is 135 miles north of Jerusalem, so this was no Sunday afternoon outing. If Saul and his followers were on foot (the Bible doesn't tell us if they were on horse-back or not) and able to walk fourteen miles a day, we're talking a ten-day trip. So Saul must have been locked and loaded to find all the Christians he could and return them to Jerusalem for "justice."

And then in a flash, he was struck by a blinding light, fell to the ground, and heard a voice from the heavens say:

> "Saul! Saul! Why are you persecuting me?"
> "Who are you, lord?" Saul asked.
> And the voice replied, "I am Jesus, the one you are perse-cuting! Now get up and go into the city, and you will be told what you must do."
> —Acts 9:4b–6 (NLT)

What happened next was a time of reordering, rebuilding, and reorganizing his life. A time of transformation. I'll have a lot more to say about transformation in my next chapter, but for the moment, let me share a few thoughts on the power of this man to impact literally billions of people over the last two thousand years.

What I love about the Apostle Paul is that he defined what success is for a leader. That definition comes through an acronym I call VPR: vision, persistence, and resilience.

Once Paul got a vision of who Jesus was, which was mercy and grace, he—much like a lawyer trained to write briefs—was able to articulate many incredible insights on what it means to have a relation-ship with God.

For instance, after he met Jesus Christ, Paul understood this beauti-ful thing called mercy. Again, Paul was a lawyer, so he knew "mercy" as a litigious term. Mercy means: *I do not get what I deserve. Even though I deserve death for my sin, because of the mercy of God, through the life of Jesus Christ, I don't have to receive the sentence of death. Instead, my sentence is dismissed, and I receive the mercy of God.*

Another way to look at mercy is to consider the story about a guy on Death Row. The governor calls the prison warden at the eleventh hour and announces he's pardoning the condemned man. A pardon means it's as though the crime never happened. The criminal's record is expunged; the crime is no longer there.

It's like if any of us were to ask God, "Do You remember what I did?"

And He would say, "No, because I pardoned you. I choose not to remember what you did."

Since Paul was the greatest teacher about grace, let's continue the metaphor about the governor pardoning the man on Death Row. When the governor commutes the sentence, he knows he was committing to setting the man free. But the man has no home. He has no car. He has no job. He has nothing.

So the governor calls back and asks to speak to the prisoner. He says, "You know that I commuted your death sentence. Now I would like to offer you something else: I would like to adopt you. You will find a limousine waiting for you with an envelope containing a key to a home as well as a job offer. A box of clothing is in the trunk." That's called grace: receiving what you don't deserve.

Mercy means not getting what you deserve, and grace means getting what you do not deserve. That's what Paul offered the Church: the understanding of the gift of God, through Jesus Christ, which is God's mercy and God's grace.

Paul's greatest challenge was that everything he loved, everything he cared about, every friend he had, every association he made, every relationship he had in the community, was cast aside after he turned his back on Judaism. He became a Christian, the very belief system he persecuted, the very thing he had thought was a cult. When he said yes to Jesus as his Messiah, he became a man without a country. The Jews didn't like him, and the Christians were leery of him because of his past deeds.

Yet Paul wrote these words: "But one thing I do: Forgetting what is behind and straining toward what is ahead, I press on toward the goal to win the prize for which God has called me heavenward in Christ Jesus" (Philippians 3:13b–14 NIV).

Because Paul held on to the vision he got from God on the Damascus road, he became one of the greatest church planters and one of the greatest writers of one of the greatest stories. He did this so that we may have vision.

◆   ◆   ◆   ◆

The second idea in my VPR acronym is *persistence*.

Paul was persistent. If he was rejected, he kept going. If he was shipwrecked, he kept going. If he was in prison, he kept going. If he was stripped of his rights, he was still determined to press ahead.

To live is Christ, to die is gain.

That gift of persistence is something Paul gave to the Church. The idea that you have to be committed. The idea that you have to look forward to being with Jesus in the next life. The idea that you have to be absolutely crazy for the things of God. Paul had that zeal. I like to call it contagious enthusiasm and contagious commitment.

One of the stories about Paul that I love to share is how he had a dream of preaching in the city of Rome. Keep in mind that Paul was also a Roman citizen, which gave him the right to travel throughout all the provinces. His dream was to be able to stand in a public square among the Seven Hills of Rome and declare, "Jesus is Lord!"

When Paul entered the Eternal City, however, he arrived in chains. He was led to a Roman dungeon and chained to a wall. I can imagine Paul saying to God, "Why would you bring me to Rome only to give me a prison cell with a small window looking out to the Seven Hills? It was my dream to preach the Gospel throughout the Roman empire, especially in the capital city, because all roads lead to Rome. But You have me captive. You have me chained up with these centurions, which means if I escape, they will be killed, so I'm not going anywhere. Oh, God. Why has this happened? Why? Why?"

We men often ask God questions like:

- *Why am I in this situation?*
- *Why is this so hard?*
- *Why am I in this particular relationship?*

When Paul cried out, God asked him a question: "What's in your hand, Paul?"

"Well, all I have is a pen and some paper," the apostle replied.

And God said, "Exactly. So use this time to write to the church of Ephesus. Use this time to write to the church of Colossae. Use this time to write to the church of Philippi. Use this time to write Philemon, a leader in the Colossian church."

But God wasn't done yet. He said to Paul, "What you would have preached in Rome would be forgotten in a week. But what you're going to write now will last for thousands of years and be read by billions of people."

And that's how the prison epistles came to be.

◆   ◆   ◆   ◆

The third and final aspect to the VPR acronym is that Paul taught us resilience. Anyone who can write the following defines what resiliency is all about:

> I have worked harder, been put in prison more often, been whipped times without number, and faced death again and again. Five different times the Jewish leaders gave me thirty-nine lashes. Three times I was beaten with rods.

Once I was stoned. Three times I was shipwrecked. Once
I spent a whole night and a day adrift at sea. I have traveled
on many long journeys. I have faced danger from rivers and
from robbers. I have faced danger from my own people, the
Jews, as well as from the Gentiles. I have faced danger in
the cities, in the deserts, and on the seas. And I have faced
danger from men who claim to be believers but are not. I
have worked hard and long, enduring many sleepless
nights. I have been hungry and thirsty and have often gone
without food. I have shivered in the cold, without enough
clothing to keep me warm.
　　—2 Corinthians 11:23b–27 (NLT)

And many of us worried about having enough toilet paper during
the coronavirus pandemic.

Paul knew what torture and physical pain felt like. But he knew
this chronic pain was temporary and that Heaven awaited him, even
though his body's pain sensors had to be screaming. "God's power is
made perfect in weakness," he wrote in his letter to the Corinthians.

There's no doubt, however, that Paul had some flaws, including
a bad temper. I say that because his anger broke up his relationship
with Barnabas for a season. At one time, they were very close. Barnabas was the guy who brought him before the early Church disciples
to vouch that he was a legitimate convert (because the disciples didn't
believe Paul was authentic). Barnabas loaned Paul his credibility. He
put his name on the line for Paul so that he would be accepted among
the brethren.

Then Paul took John Mark to task after he showed some cowardice
in various situations. Paul said, "Get him away from me. He has no
value. He's a chicken." What Paul forgot to understand was John Mark
was Barnabas's nephew, so this was going to create tension and a rift.

Barnabas said, "No, no, no. We're not getting rid of him. He has value." He stood up to Paul, which caused a rift that lasted many, many years because Paul had a tough streak. Eventually he was remorseful.

At the end of his life, Paul told Timothy to bring John Mark with him because he had much to offer for the work of God. Because of Paul's resilience to bounce back from his own issues, he taught us to be forgiving and how to give a guy a second chance.

Because of Paul's action, John Mark was preserved and became a key member of the early Church. For instance, John Mark became the first person to write about the life and teaching of Jesus Christ. The Gospel of Mark is our oldest gospel and was used as a source by Matthew and Luke when they wrote their own gospels. Bottom line: without Paul and his ability to be forgiving and restorative, we wouldn't have the Gospel of Mark.

We can learn from what Paul taught us about vision, persistence, and resilience. We can be reminded that if God can change a life so radically as He did Paul's, then He can and will do the same for all of us.

When it comes to the power of one man, Paul is our blueprint, an example of how God can save anyone in rebellion against Him.

Paul's legacy is the power of the pen. Noah's legacy is the power of a hammer. Joseph's legacy is the power of a dream. Abraham's legacy is the power to heed God's instructions. David's legacy is the power of a rock.

Do you see how God can use each and every one of us? Life is like a beautifully constructed, old-fashioned Swiss watch. If you happen to open the back of one, you will see chaos—multiple gears. Some are large, some are medium-sized, some are small, some are moving rapidly, some are moving ordinarily, some are moving slowly, some are moving counterclockwise, some are moving clockwise, and some are oscillating back and forth.

Trying to understand the seemingly chaotic movement of all these pieces can drive one insane. But when you take a panoramic view, you see that all these gears, both big and small, fast and slow, are working to do one thing, which is to move the second hand one tick at a time, to move forward in the dispensation of time.

That is how God works. Everything in our lives moves like a Swiss watch: some events move quickly, while some events move slowly. Some events feel like they take life backward, while other events feel like we're moving forward, making progress. Then there are the events we don't understand—events that oscillate, go counterclockwise, or go clockwise.

If we try to understand the minutia of it all, we'll get lost. We become like a blind man in a dark room, chasing black cats who simply are not there. We spend our time chasing after confusing activities that promise a sense of accomplishment but rarely work out or last that long.

But if you can, by faith, step back and look at all the creative power that's unleashed by the events and people around you, then you will understand Paul's words in Ephesians 5:15–16 (ESV) so much better:

> Look carefully then how you walk, not as unwise but as wise,
> making the best use of the time, because the days are evil.

Notice Paul's use of the word *time* in this Scripture. The Greek word that he used for "time" was *kairos*, which signifies an appointed time or opportune moment for action.

That's different from the other Greek word for *time*, which is *chronos* and refers to minutes and seconds.

We tend to think of our time as *chronos* because we manage our lives by the clock: pick up the kids from school at 3:00 p.m., work out with a personal trainer at 5:00 p.m., dinner at 7:00 p.m., and lights out by 10:00 p.m. Our lives are dictated and controlled by this time, which isn't a bad thing.

Being conscious of the time is a good thing. Psalm 90:12 (NIV) says, "Teach us to number our days, that we may gain a heart of wisdom."

God is the magnificent Watchmaker who knows how to use both *chronos* and *kairos* to move you forward. What I want you to look for is having a *kairos* mindset. Joseph, for example, was seventeen years old when he was sold into bondage in Egypt and was separated from his father for the next thirteen years. Instead of lamenting that lost time, he let God use it in incredible ways that led Joseph into Pharaoh's palace, where he was able to save his family—and thus the Hebrew nation—during an intense famine.

So take the time when God calls you.

Paul could have resisted the call when he was blinded on the road to Damascus. He could have run from it like Jonah did, but Paul took the time when God showed up in his life. Every man will have a *kairos* moment. Think of the burning bush of Moses, the anointing of David by Samuel, the voice from God to Abraham.

Sometimes God will step into time to change your time for all time. This is what He did with the burning bush, the anointing of a shepherd boy's head with oil, and how He blinded Paul on the road to Damascus. God moved supernaturally in the lives of these men, so prepare yourself for what He has ahead for you to do. The call could come from a sermon, from a speaker at a men's retreat, from a book you read, from a song you hear, or from a movie you watch. Whatever the medium, this call will give you an epiphany that God wants more of you and more *from* you. In other words, He wants to *transform* you.

Again, I'll have a lot more to say about transformation in my next chapter, but for now, I want to close with a poem I first shared from the pulpit when I started preaching at sixteen years old. It's called "No Time, No Time."

I knelt to pray, but not for long for I had too much to do.
Must hurry off and get to work for my bills would soon be
*   due.*
And so I said a hurried prayer and jumped up from my knees.
My Christian duty was now done, my soul could be at ease.
All through the day I had no time to speak a word of cheer.
No time to speak of Christ to a friend, they'd laugh at me,
*   I feared.*
No time, no time. That was my constant cry.
No time to give to those in need, alas it was my time to die.
And when before the Lord I came, I stood with downcast
*   eyes.*
Within His hands He held a book. It was the Book of Life.
God, looking through His book, said your name I cannot
*   find.*
I was once going to write it down, God said, but I never
*   found the time.*

◆   ◆   ◆   ◆

Discussion Questions

1. What shame still has you in prison?
2. Are you more concerned about your reputation than your character? Why is that?
3. Have you had a "road to Damascus" experience? What was that like?
4. When Jesus showed up in your life, how did it change you?
5. When Paul was in prison, wanting to preach, God gave him a pen to change the world. What is in your hand that you can give to God to begin to change yourself and those around you?

PART III

Transformation

8

The Power of Transformation

When I was growing up, I had a severe stuttering problem. It was awful, especially in the classroom, where I was petrified to open my mouth.

If a substitute teacher called on me and asked me for my name, I sounded like an old car trying to turn over on a cold winter morning: *rrrr-rrrr...rrrr-rrrr...rrrr-ron...aaarcherrrr.*

Even worse was when I had to say words that started with the letter *s*. If I did manage to sound out some *ssss-ssss*-syll-ables, spit would come flying out. I'm telling you, I was a mess in more ways than one. No wonder I dreaded going to school, where my classmates teased me mercilessly in the yard during recess.

I mentioned earlier that Mrs. Spears was the kind-hearted school-teacher who heard about my plight and offered to help me overcome my stuttering when the school day ended. Each afternoon, she put me through a series of exercises that emphasized making certain sounds like *lee*, *la*, and *lo* as well as *see*, *saw*, and *sir*. I was especially excited to work on my *s* sounds because even saying short words like *sure* tripped me up.

Mrs. Spears knew the right formula, and after a couple of months of after-school lessons, I stopped ducking my head when my fourth-grade schoolteacher asked if anyone knew what the capital of Nebraska was. Instead, I raised my hand proudly to be called on because I knew I could say "Lincoln," without getting stuck on the opening consonant.

I tell this story because overcoming stuttering changed *everything* for me. No longer was I a wallflower, hoping my teacher wouldn't look my way or single me out. No longer was I left behind in the classroom. No longer was I one of the worst students. No longer was I laughed at.

Instead, I was transformed into a confident young student who *wanted* to be heard, who *wanted* to make great grades, who *wanted* to make something of himself. My transformation rewired my mind, which changed everything about how I viewed myself or what I thought was possible.

Paul wrote about this transformation of the mind in one of his greatest teachings:

> Do not conform to the pattern of this world, but be transformed by the renewing of your mind. Then you will be able to test and approve what God's will is—his good, pleasing and perfect will.
> —Romans 12:2 (NIV)

The central theme of this final section of this book is that *before* you can change your family, *before* you can change your church, *before* you can change your community, you have to change yourself. If you're caught in the throes of addiction, if you're an alcoholic, if you're verbally abusive to others, I first want you to focus on your mind and what you think about. The first step to renewing your mind is to become more like Christ, which, as Paul said, is an ever-ongoing process. This is more difficult than it sounds because it's never easy to change thoughts, beliefs, and habits formed over decades. If there's anything we can agree on, it's that we know there's a battle for our minds that's constant and unrelenting.

Much of that stems from the way we are wired and made by God. For instance:

Men are visual.

Men are responsive.

Men are reactive.

That's why it's hard to turn our eyes from shapely women, especially when they are dressed provocatively on the street—or, more seriously, naked in a porn video. Unless we renew our minds to be more like the mind of Christ, we're going to find ourselves constantly falling into the trap of pornography. That's the *opposite* of renewing our minds. We can do better. I know we can because I've studied how

Words to Live By

"For as he thinks in his heart, so is he...."
(Proverbs 23:7a NKJV)

"Death and life are in the power of the tongue...."
(Proverbs 18:21a NASB)

"Let this mind be in you which was also in Christ Jesus...."
(Philippians 2:5 NKJV)

"Whether you think you can, or you think you can't you're right."
—Henry Ford, founder of the Ford Motor Company

"You see things and you say 'Why?' But I dream things that never were and I say 'Why not?'"
—George Bernard Shaw, playwright

"The only thing worse than being blind is having sight but no vision."
—Helen Keller, deaf and blind author

minds transform and have shared this information throughout my corporate career and speaking ministry.

When I attended Baldwin Wallace University in Berea, Ohio, I enjoyed studying how the mind could be changed to impact the body and alter behaviors, as well as the science behind the psychology of transformational leadership. A few years later, I accepted a junior management position with the Eaton Corporation and was put in charge of transforming organizational systems at several of its manufacturing plants in North America. I was also leading by implementing a self-directed work team system to facilitate high performance.

One time, my superiors sent me to the Pacific Institute in Seattle, founded by a remarkable man and high school football coach named Lou Tice. His company specialized in leadership development with the goal of educating and empowering individuals to an ever-greater commitment to making a better world.

Lou was an incredible speaker—I could see why he was a successful high school football coach at one time—whose mantra was: *Before you can change a corporation, you must first change the individual.* Lou and his associates helped me understand how the mind works to change habits and attitudes.

One of the ways the mind works is through something called the "four stages of competence." These four stages are:

1. Unconscious incompetence
2. Conscious incompetence
3. Conscious competence
4. Unconscious competence

The first stage, unconscious incompetence, is when our blind spots are still blind and we're blissfully ignorant of what's holding us back. I liken it to this sentence: *You don't know what you don't know.* Or said another way: *You don't yet know what you can't do.*

Examples of unconscious incompetence are things you do automatically, like rocking on your heels during a sales presentation. You aren't aware that you're rocking back and forth until someone tells you. Or you might crack your knuckles before a big test or regularly mispronounce a word without any idea you're doing it wrong. Other people can see your error, but you can't.

Next is conscious incompetence, which is when you've become aware of something that needs to shift or change, but that shift hasn't happened yet. You may have the desire to change, but you're feeling stuck. Conscious incompetence is when you're doing something wrong and know you're doing it wrong.

Third is conscious competence, which means you've made a change, taken on learning a new skill, or are striving toward a new quality in your character, but it's not second nature yet. This would be like when you were learning to drive. Your instructor reminds you to look in the rearview mirror often, be ready to take your foot off the gas and place it on the brake, and not talk to anyone else in the vehicle, but those actions aren't second nature. Conscious competence is when you're doing something right, but you have to consciously focus on doing it the right way.

Finally, there is unconscious competence, where you've adopted a new skill, a new mindset, a new way of doing things, and it's happening automatically. You don't have to think about it; it naturally occurs. Unconscious competence is when you're doing something right, and you don't even have to think about it.

I've made an attempt to become unconsciously competent in the most important areas of my life. When I've chosen to adopt certain lifestyles and behaviors, I want them to be so ingrained in my being that I don't have to consciously think about them anymore.

For instance, I've made it a point when I'm angry to count to ten before I speak. I've made it a point to drink water instead of alcohol or soft drinks. I've made it a point to eat healthy foods before I gravitate to sweets. I've made it a point to be forgiving instead of holding a grudge. I've made it a point to be open to new ideas and not reject people who don't think like me. Being unconsciously competent is part of my DNA, part of my breathing, part of my thinking. It's who I am now.

What's the key to becoming unconsciously competent?

Answering that question is the focus of this chapter because it helps explain the concept of being transformed by the mind of Christ, of becoming a transformed nonconformist. When you're transformed, you can tap into the power of one man.

Paul was certainly a transformed nonconformist, the Pharisee-turned-believer-in-Jesus who received the wrath of his fellow Jews as well as the powerful people who were in charge: the Romans. In those days, those who didn't conform to either powerful entity were pressured to shut up and were threatened with torture and execution—from stoning to crucifixion. Those dangers didn't stop Paul from urging Christians to become nonconformists as far as the world's systems were concerned.

To go deeper—and to begin to answer the question of how to become unconsciously competent—let's talk about the conscious process of thought. I've prepared a graphic that will aid in this discussion.

Notice the first cloud in the upper left corner: reality.

Based upon the theory of self-concept in human psychology, we don't see things as they actually are. We see things as *we* are. That is our reality. We view reality through a prism that's formed by our life experiences and significant emotional events. We view reality in a very specific way that affects our emotions and our actions.

Here's an example of what I mean.

Typically, a white suburban male going for a walk close to home will look at a police officer cruising through the neighborhood as a compatriot, as a neighbor, or just as someone doing his job. An urban black kid growing up in the ghetto of Cleveland, however, will see

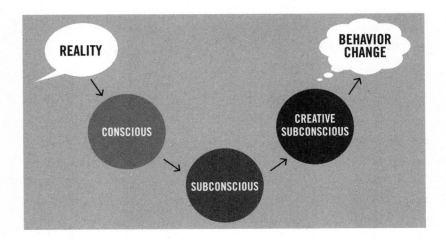

that cop in a whole different light. He will see the police officer as an outsider, someone who can destroy his life, someone who could send him to prison for the slightest infraction, or even someone who could draw a gun and shoot him to death.

Same guy, same uniform, same reality, but based upon the urban kid's perception and emotional experiences in life, he interprets a cop cruising the streets completely differently than a white kid living in the suburbs. This perception always hardens into reality.

In order for you to change how you act toward others, such as the cop on a beat, you must change the way you perceive things. To do that, you must be aware that you actually perceive things in a particular way.

The way we perceive things has always fascinated me, which is why I would like to share a little exercise with you. Please read the following sentence one time, thoroughly and quickly:

> Finished files are the result of many years of scientific study
> of many studies of many years.

Now go back and count the number of *F*s you see. Write that number down.

Now go back and count the number of times that you see "of" and then count the number of Fs.

What did you discover?

The first time through, I'm willing to wager that you saw two, three, or four Fs when there were actually seven in the sentence.

Why did you miss the other Fs?

The reason that people often fail to see the others is because the brain locks out information or stimuli in our environment based upon past conditioning. First of all, the letter F usually makes the "*ffff*" sound, like in the word "fox." But in the word "of", the letter F makes a "*vvv*" sound. Since you've been conditioned to sound your words out phonetically, starting in first and second grade, you've probably read the word "of" so many times in your life that you process it as one unit, overlooking the second letter/sound.

The lesson again is about perception and how we do not see things as they are, but tend to see things as we are.

Consider this graph that I use in my presentations:

There are two key ideas behind this tool:

1. That individuals can build trust with each other by disclosing information about themselves
2. That individuals can learn about themselves and come to terms with personal issues with feedback from others

The first step to having a true breakthrough in knowing yourself is to understand that you have blind spots—scientifically known as *scotomas*. You don't and can't see everything. You need other people you trust to see things that you cannot see.

Can you see what is directly behind you as you're looking straight ahead? Of course not. But a person standing with his or her back to yours can see what you cannot.

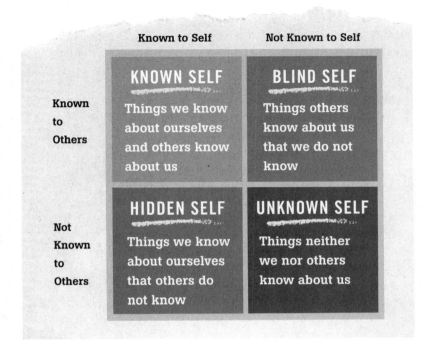

That's one of the reasons why—when God created Adam—He proclaimed it was not good that man should be alone. The wisest man who ever lived, Solomon, said two are better than one (Ecclesiastes 4:9).

One of the greatest barriers to success, however, is a *psychological scotoma*, which means that if something happens or if there is information that's inconvenient or not considered "good news," the mind responds by turning a "blind eye" to it and blocking out that information based upon past conditioning. In other words, when you look at something or have something happen to you, you won't be able to see it, based upon your conditioning. Instead, you lock on and you lock out. I call this *lo-lo* for short.

Once you lock on to a perception of something, you lock out the alternative. If you're white and lock on to the belief that blacks are dangerous, you lock them out of becoming your friends. If you're black and lock on to the belief that whites are racist, you lock out the idea that they can be very good people.

- Once you lock on to saying "I'm a loser..."
- Once you lock on to saying "I'm an alcoholic..."
- Once you lock on to saying, "I'm a failure..."
- Once you lock on to saying, "I'm weak..."
- Once you lock on to saying, "Daddy was right..."
- Once you lock on to saying, "I'll never have any money..."
- Once you lock on to saying, "I'll always have relationship challenges..."

I could go on, but once you lock on to something, you often lock out any possibility that an alternative could exist. This is why I say that reality is understanding that you do not see things as they are, but you see things as *you* are, the epitome of the lock-on, lock-out syndrome.

My grandfather possessed a psychological scotoma. For years, he had a real blind spot when it came to Christianity because of his experiences with white Christians in the South. He saw cross burnings. He saw white Christians dragging black men out of houses. He saw lynchings. He saw white Christians burn down black churches. He saw white Christians blowing up 16th Street Baptist Church in Birmingham, Alabama, killing four little black girls.

Based upon these evil experiences, can you blame my grandfather for believing that Christians as well as the Bible and a white Jesus were to be avoided? His perceptions hardened after he was sentenced to prison and his white father-in-law told his wife that being married to a black person was an evil sin. His father-in-law's question—"What does light have to do with darkness?"—reinforced the idea that religion was evil, a perception that filtered down to my grandfather's children.

So how could my grandfather's mind—or anyone else's, for that matter—be changed or transformed under those circumstances? How can any of us put these personal perceptions aside and tap into the power of one man?

For answers, it would be useful if I start by describing what the conscious thought process looks like. It has four functions:

- Perception
- Association
- Evaluation
- Decision

I've already talked about perception, about how we do not see things as they are but rather as we are, which stems from our ethnocentric ideological backgrounds and life experiences. For us, reality is incorporated through our five senses: what we see, what we smell, what we feel, what we hear, and what we touch. These five senses record and edit what we are seeing based upon our scotomas, our paradigms, and our life experiences.

Once you perceive something and ingest it into your conscious mind, you make an immediate association. *Have I heard this before? Have I tasted this before? Have I smelled this before? Have I felt this before?* Your answers help you associate the experience with everything you've been through in life up to that point.

For instance, I remember when I traveled to South Africa for the first time. "Oh my gosh—this country reminds me of Germany and being in Europe," I told my hosts. My experiences in Johannesburg and Cape Town made me feel as though I truly was not in Africa.

The reason I felt this was because the Dutch and the British colonized South Africa, which meant that they brought their culture as well as their architecture. The country, at that time, was dominated by whites of European ancestry.

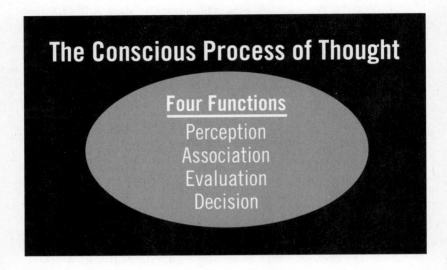

I've returned to South Africa a couple of times since the apartheid era ended. Unfortunately, South Africa is beginning to look more like impoverished Africa since the African National Congress came to power.

The next time you step into a new environment, ask yourself what you're comparing it to. This association will tell you everything you need to know about your background and your beliefs.

The third step, after perceiving something and then associating it with past experiences, is to do an evaluation: *Is this good or is it bad? Is this true or is it false?*

We see this in how we choose what news sources to watch, listen to, or read. My conservative friends immediately say anything from the "lamestream media"—CNN, MSNBC, the *New York Times*, or the *Washington Post*—is fake news, without question. But if the story comes from Fox News, it's the gospel truth.

My liberal friends feel the opposite way, telling me that anything from Fox News is right-wing propaganda and the only trusted sources of information come from media giants like the *New York Times* or one of the three major networks. They've made an evaluation that opinions or news stories broadcast on Fox News can't possibly be true.

If you want a great example of evaluation, I present O.J. Simpson, who was charged with the murders of his ex-wife, Nicole Brown Simpson, and her friend Ron Goldman over twenty-five years ago. If you're of a certain age, then you remember what defense attorney Johnnie Cochran told the jury while holding up a pair of leather gloves that Simpson had allegedly worn on the night of the murders: "If it doesn't fit, you must acquit." Simpson famously struggled to put on one of the gloves during the trial.

When the not-guilty verdict was read on October 3, 1995, black people applauded and danced in the streets. White people cried out, "Oh my God! It's an injustice! All the evidence, the blood, and the knife!" The not-guilty verdict divided the country by race.

Here's my take on why that happened. For openers, the majority of black people I know believe O.J. *did* commit the horrific murders, so they weren't clapping for his acquittal. They were clapping for this reason: *White America, now you know what it feels like when people are guilty and the system lets them off.*

Because that's what had happened for hundreds of years in this country. Think of all the lynchings in the South and black people in Alabama and Mississippi getting murdered. The culprits would be caught and go to trial. They were guilty as hell, but after all the evidence was presented, an all-white jury would acquit them. Time and time again this happened.

Andrew Young, a black congressman from Atlanta who became the U.S. ambassador to the United Nations during the Carter administration, said it best after O.J.'s acquittal: "They framed a guilty man."

This is what evaluation is all about. You see an event, and immediately you evaluate it. For example, men who've been abused by their fathers have a hard time viewing God as a loving father. They struggle with it. They associate God, who's our heavenly Father, with their earthly fathers, and the comparison is often unfavorable. *You know what? I don't want nothing to do with any more fathers.*

Evaluations happen in nanoseconds. We make a conscious decision for fight or flight, to accept or reject, to be open or closed, to continue on one path or change to another.

That's when decisions are made. And then, there's usually no turning back.

◆   ◆   ◆   ◆

Now let's turn to the first circle, labeled "conscious."

I begin with a reminder that the human mind has three ways of processing information: the conscious, the subconscious, and the creative subconscious. All three work together to control our behaviors in the real world.

As we go through life, we make conscious decisions:

Yes, that's right.

No, that's wrong.

Yes, that hurts.

No, that feels good.

These affirmations are either a statement of fact or a belief that can be either positive or negative.

"I am great" is an affirmation.

"I'm so stupid" is an affirmation.

"I'm loving" is an affirmation.

"I hate those people" is an affirmation.

"I love God" is an affirmation.

"God is so cruel" is an affirmation.

When I was working to overcome my stuttering, I wrote down the following ten sentences and vowed to repeat them every day for twenty-eight days as a way to replace old negative thinking. Here's what I read each morning and evening:

1. I am a great communicator
2. I speak slowly and clearly
3. I am calm and confident when I speak
4. I am dynamic and powerful when I speak
5. I am relaxed and at ease when I communicate
6. I feel great when I get up to speak in public
7. I am a child of God, and greater is He that is in me
8. I can do all things through Christ who strengthens me
9. I am more than a conqueror
10. I am anointed by God to share His work with love, grace, kindness, and mercy

Do you see how positive each affirmation was? No wonder my confidence soared. When I speak today before audiences, I love sharing the following ideas, which always bring a strong response:

- If you can control a man's thinking, you do not have to worry about his actions
- When you determine what a man shall think, you do not have to concern yourself about what he will do
- If you make a man feel that he is inferior, you do not have to compel him to accept an inferior status, for he will seek it himself
- If you make a man think that he is just an outcast, you do not have to order him to the back door. He will go without being told, and if there is no back door, his very nature will demand one

This is why I always wince when I hear someone say "I'm so stupid" after making a mistake. When they say it with passion, it goes somewhere. It doesn't disappear into the universe as a vapor. What happens is that it gets transmitted as a truth to the next circle, the subconscious.

The subconscious mind is like the CPU of a computer, the central processing unit. It is like a servomechanism, an automatic device used to correct the performance of a mechanism by means of error-sensing feedback. Examples are automatic machine tools, satellite-track antennas, and automatic navigation systems. Similarly, the subconscious mind cannot tell the difference between an actual experience and one that you vividly imagined. Both are recorded as real.

There's a formula for how affirmations impact the subconscious, and it goes like this: $I \ x \ V = RSL$, or Imagination times Vividness equals Reality on a Subconscious Level.

Have you ever dreamed that you're falling, and the dream is so vivid and so real that your body physically reacts to it by moving, jumping, or shifting? That's the subconscious at work, a place where you store all your experiences and images.

One of the most tragic things that I deal with in my ministry to black America is the hidden reality of self-hatred. Many black people *hate* being black and *hate* the connotation of what it means to be black.

The example I'm going to give you comes from a study done by black psychologists Kenneth and Mamie Clark regarding the psychological effects of segregation on African American children. These became known as the "doll tests."

In this study, which was conducted in the late 1940s and early 1950s, four dolls, identical except for color, were used to test children's racial perceptions. Black children between the ages of three and seven were asked:

- Which doll do you prefer to play with?
- Which doll is the pretty doll?
- Which doll is the smart doll?

A majority of the black children pointed to the white doll.

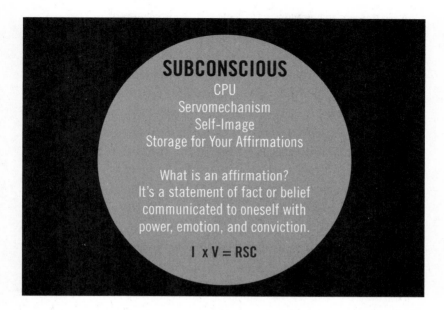

When the black children were asked, "Which doll is stupid?" they pointed to the black doll 80 percent of the time. When asked which doll was most like them, they'd point to the brown doll and say, "That's a nigger. I'm a nigger."

Their findings were used to support the plaintiffs in *Brown v. Board of Education of Topeka*, the historic 1954 U.S. Supreme Court decision declaring that state laws establishing racial segregation in the public schools were unconstitutional. This landmark decision overturned an 1896 Supreme Court ruling, *Plessy v. Ferguson*, in which the court said that racially segregated public facilities were legal, as long as the facilities for whites and blacks were equal.

So where did five-year-old kids learn that their own race was ugly, stupid, bad, and ignorant? Answer: from the reality around them.

But Ron, that happened seventy years ago! Surely things have changed in the black community.

Not so fast.

That same experiment was done in 2010 by a black graduate student to see how far we've come since 1954. Now, you would think with the civil rights movement, all the sit-ins, all the choruses of "We Shall Overcome," and all of these advancements in race relations with a black president and all the black governors, mayors, and sports superstars like LeBron James, Michael Jordan, Tiger Woods, Arthur Ashe, and Serena and Venus Williams, you could confidently assume that the results of the "doll test" would be different.

The results were different, all right. They were worse.

The self-hatred of being black has grown over time because beauty is still viewed through a white lens. As an example, in the black community, there's an important question that always gets asked sooner or later: "Do you have good hair or bad hair?"

If your hair is more like white people's hair, then it's straighter, maybe with a bit of a wave. That's what we call "good hair" in the black community. If your hair is kinky, tight, and coarse, it's called "bad hair." The issue is so prevalent that most black girls won't go in the swimming pool because they don't want to get their hair wet. Instead, most black girls get a perm and use a comb with lye to straighten out the kinks. So when you see black women with straight hair, that's not natural. A chemical process is used to straighten their hair.

This same mindset extends to skin color. Among black people, if your skin is lighter in color, you're better off. If you have light skin, you're smarter, you're prettier. But if your skin is darker, you're ugly. You have no future.

This is even true in Africa, where black people have been conditioned to believe white is beautiful, white is right, white is good, and white is preferred. This attitude dates back to the time of slavery. If a slave had a lighter skin tone and looked like the master—often because the master had raped one of his female slaves—that offspring became preferred.

Those slaves went into the house. They didn't have to be in the sun. They didn't have to work the fields. They got the good jobs. They worked in the kitchen, they shined the silverware, they were chambermaids and valets. But if they were dark-skinned, they were out in the fields from sunup to sundown, getting whipped if they didn't work hard enough or copped an attitude.

The whole point is the power of perception, the power of suggestion, and the power of affirmation when it comes to the subconscious mind. This can happen in the white community as well when a white mother tells her son, "You're just like your father—a bum who left us on the street. You're a loser just like him. You're no good at all." The boy who hears this affirms her statement in his mind: *Mom's right. I'm like my father and no good to anybody.*

A classic example happened when the Hebrews were enslaved in Egypt. For hundreds of years, they were filthy, dirty slaves. The Egyptians were wealthy, powerful, and successful. For ten generations, the Hebrews learned that being Hebrew was bad. They learned that being Hebrew was dirty. They learned that being Hebrew was *less than.*

And then Moses arrived on the scene, and through the hand of God, the Hebrew people were set free by ten miraculous plagues, the death of Pharaoh's son, and the opening of the Red Sea. Now you would think after all these miracles that the Hebrew nation would be transformed forever and be loyal to God.

Yet as soon as they were out in the desert and a crisis came up, they grumbled and said, "Were there no graves in Egypt, that you brought us out to the desert to die? Stone him!"

Why did the Hebrews turn against Moses so quickly and thus against God? Because people in general would rather hold on to a known pain or misery than pursue an unknown possibility that could be good. It's one of the reasons why 75 percent of black men who go to prison and are then released end up right back in a jail cell—it's a life they know. It's why drug addicts go back to putting poison in their bodies after thirty days of rehab—it's a lifestyle they know.

The challenge for God was not taking the Hebrews out of Egypt. That was the easy part. The challenge was taking Egypt out of the Hebrews. They still had the mentality that they were slaves, that they were less than.

Even when they finally reached the Promised Land and God gave them tremendous military victories under Joshua's leadership, within *one generation* His people turned to worship other gods—the god Baal, the Philistines' god, the Canaanites' god, the Jebusites' god—because they wanted to be something else.

I could go on—remember, I'm a preacher who loves to teach—but I say all this to bring forth this point: change begins with one man changing his mindset. That's the power of one man.

Let me illustrate this by telling a story about the thousandth monkey. In Africa at one time, a pesticide called DDT was used to kill insects that were destroying the crops. Farmers who wanted to eat their own fruit knew that because of the toxins in DDT, they would have to take their fruit down to the river and rinse it off thoroughly before they ate it so they wouldn't get sick. The monkeys, however, would steal some of the produce from the farm. They'd eat it and die because DDT was on it.

One monkey—just one—observed the farmers and how they would take the produce down to the river, rinse it off, eat it, and not die. So this one monkey mimicked what he saw. After he stole some fruit, he took it down to the river and washed it. He did not die. He did this again, again, and again.

The other monkeys watched him. The next day, two monkeys did it. They lived. The next day, four. The next day, sixteen. The next day, thirty-two. The next day, sixty-four. When the thousandth monkey washed off his food and ate it, the level of consciousness was raised immediately in the entire monkey community. And that became the new paradigm. Every monkey, when he stole his fruit, ran to the river, washed it off, ate it, and lived. But it all started with one monkey.

Change can start with one man, who can wash his mind of evil and self-hate. And then a second guy, then a fourth guy, then a sixteenth. And it grows until the thousandth man. Now you have generational change, a community change—but it starts with the power of one man deciding to wash his mind.

◆   ◆   ◆   ◆

Going back to the second circle, labeled "subconscious," think about a garden.

What is something nobody wants in their garden?

Weeds.

I have an acronym for weeds: *Wrong Emotional Experiences Destroy Self-esteem.*

Nobody plants weeds. Nobody goes out buying weed seeds. Weeds are so powerful that they show up without invitation. Weeds are so strong that they'll even grow between cracks in a sidewalk.

Similarly, negative thoughts are like weeds: they are powerful and take deep root in our brains and in our emotions. Negative thoughts are far more powerful than positive ones. Research tells us that it takes eight positive affirmations to overcome one negative one.

When I talk to football coaches who've been coaching for a while, I hear them say, "It's no longer the exhilaration of winning that motivates me, Ron. It's the fear of losing. I hate the feeling of losing so much that I coach better. But I don't enjoy the wins like I used to. I win, and the game is over. A win is what I'm supposed to do. But when I lose, the result lingers like a skunk smell."

Every time my stepfather told me I was stupid, that I was a stutterer, that I was a bed-wetter, a weed sprouted in my mind. In fact, whenever I relive those moments, I hear Dick Archer's voice, which plants another weed in my subconscious mind. Weeds spread rapidly, like cancer. Negative thoughts spread rapidly in our emotions and in our minds.

Now as any person who likes gardening will tell you, the key to ridding gardens of weeds permanently is getting the roots out. It doesn't do any good to hit them with a weed whacker. They'll be back in two weeks.

When negative thoughts aren't rooted out, self-destructive behavior is certain to return. This is why so many people never get past their past. They allow these negative experiences they've focused on—that they've affirmed, that they've relived with emotion and conviction—to spread and choke out the good thoughts.

Consequently, they find a way to mess up. They find a way to be self-destructive. *Yeah. That's more like me. Yeah. That's who I am. Yeah. I'm not that good.*

And they go back to what's always been normal for them. That's the power of the subconscious mind.

◆   ◆   ◆   ◆

Now I'd like to move on to the third circle, which is the "creative subconscious."

The creative subconscious has two purposes: the first is to maintain sanity, and the second is to make sure what you say to yourself privately comes out in your behavior publicly.

Sanity is not being normal per se. Sanity is making sure that who you say you are privately is reflected by what you do publicly. If you view yourself as a failure and you're successful, however, that's being insane because your thoughts don't match the picture reality presents. If you have a good relationship with someone (like a spouse) but believe you don't deserve it, that's effectively insanity.

It's like if you are a drinker and you make a promise to stop drinking. You follow through on your promise and stop drinking. Life gets better, as it should. But your mind says, *Wait a minute. That's not who you are. You don't deserve this. This is not your truth.*

When that happens, you have to find a way to get back to where you belong. It's like when you're released from prison but you still believe you're a prisoner. How many times have we heard about ex-cons doing something stupid, like shoplifting, and winding up behind bars again?

If you've been belittled by people and by life and you affirm it, but then you have a breakthrough, it's likely you won't believe you deserve it. You'll think that you lucked out, that this really isn't you. You'll live your entire life afraid of being revealed as an imposter, that this is not really who you are.

So let me ask this question: How many people who are poor or working-class win the lottery and go back to being poor—or worse—within a few years?

Statistics vary from one-third to 70 percent of lottery winners ending up losing it all, but everyone agrees that lottery winners have great trouble with overnight riches. There's a strong chance that in three to five years all the money will be gone, and they'll be worse off.

I contend that many lottery winners really don't believe they deserve the winning ticket and act accordingly. They had a poverty mindset before, so they found a way to get back to where they think they belong. There's a term for this: *gestalt*. This German word refers to perception and means something that is made of many parts and yet is somehow more than or different from the combination of its parts.

So let's say you have an old kitchen and your wife likes it. After years in this kitchen, she knows how to use it and cooks delicious meals and makes wonderful desserts and all that. This is her kitchen, her domain, and she has no complaints because this is all she knows.

Then you're invited to a friend's house for dinner, and they show off their remodeled kitchen. White shaker cabinets, stainless

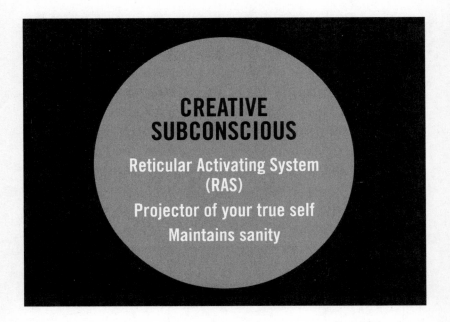

CREATIVE
SUBCONSCIOUS
Reticular Activating System
(RAS)
Projector of your true self
Maintains sanity

steel appliances, gorgeous Corian countertops, striking tile back-splash, a large island, and new flooring in dark wood. What an amazing kitchen.

Then your wife comes back to her old kitchen, the one with a faded linoleum floor, chipped tiles on the countertops, and appliances that were around when Reagan was president. Her old kitchen is no longer acceptable to her. "I can't cook here anymore," she says.

"But you were cooking here yesterday," you reply.

But now she's affirmed that she deserves a new kitchen and won't be happy until she gets a remodeled one. That's *gestalt*, meaning you've had an experience and think you truly deserve it.

Now that I've shared how to utilize the conscious, the subconscious, and the creative subconscious as you move toward unconsciously competent behavior, it's your turn to try it out. Here's a formula for establishing a goal, using the SMART method:

- The goal has to be **Specific**
- The goal has to be **Measurable**
- The goal has to be **Attainable**
- The goal has to be **Relevant**
- And the goal has to have a **Timeline**

Once you write down your goal, add ten affirmations about it that make you feel alive, energetic, and purposeful.

If you said, "I want to lose weight," that's a nice thought, but not a goal. But if you say, "Starting on the day after the Fourth of July, I would like to lose twenty pounds, accomplishing it by December 15," that's a goal because it's specific, it's measurable, it's attainable, it's relevant, and there's a timeline.

The reason I like writing down affirmations regarding the goal is because affirmations make you feel alive, make you feel energetic, and make you feel purposeful. Affirmations are the software that control the three consciousnesses that make you act like the person you want to be without having to think about it. Since the goal is to get to unconscious competence, these affirmations can help you visualize and affirm changes in your life. I recommend that you read these affirmations for twenty-eight days straight, until you don't have to think about what you want to achieve. Twenty-eight days are necessary to form a new habit.

Your affirmations must be in first person and in present tense, which will make it easier for you visualize. Here are some examples:

1. I love being fit and weighing 175 pounds
2. I am a committed and passionate person of fitness
3. I enjoy eating whole foods
4. I love walking thirty minutes a day
5. I feel so good when I step on the scale and find I weigh less than I did before

Read these affirmations in the morning after you wake up and then again before you go to bed. You can print them out and fold the piece of paper in your Bible or tape it to the mirror in your bathroom. Whether it's for losing weight, committing to a thirty-minute walk each day, saving $250 a month, or being a more loving husband, writing down these affirmations will remind you that you're on the road to forming a new habit and a new lifestyle. This will help you turn your affirmation into a belief, into an attitude, into an action, and into a habit. That's how transformation takes place.[1]

Here's another takeaway: When you start affirming for yourself more and more—*I'm a winner, I'm successful, I'm lean and mean, I'm a good husband*—suddenly the old image of you is no longer acceptable. The creative subconscious kicks in and gives you energy and ideas. Your perception of what you should be changes and your behavior begins to change and forge a new reality.

This is what Paul meant when he wrote about the renewing of your mind, as well as when he wrote this to the Philippians (4:8 NIV):

> Finally, brothers and sisters, whatever is true, whatever is noble, whatever is right, whatever is pure, whatever is lovely, whatever is admirable—if anything is excellent or praiseworthy—think about such things.

Paul didn't say think about bad things or failure or death. He said it right there: think about things that are right and good and admirable. So in order for your subconscious mind to go this route, you must think in first person: *I am this* or *I am that* . . .

It's a powerful concept that God used to introduce Himself to Moses when He said, "I am." With that simple statement, He affirmed Himself in the present tense.

I am the all-existing One. I am Me.

Then Jesus did the same thing when He said, *I am the good shepherd. I am the true vine. I am the door. I am the way, the truth, and the life. I am the living water. I am the bread of life.*

Over and over again, He affirmed who He was in first-person language that was experiential and contained positive imagery. He didn't say, *I will be.* He didn't say, *I want to be.* He didn't say, *I could be.* He said everything in the present tense because the subconscious mind only believes what you tell it in the first person, not when you tell it what you want to be.

I urge you to think in the present tense because yesterday is history. Tomorrow is yet a mystery. Today is a gift; that's why it's called the present. All we ever really have is now; it'll always be now. It will never be tomorrow. So be nice now. Be good now. Be forgiving now.

Because all you will ever have in your life is now.

9

One Man's Story:
Jesus Christ, the Son of God

When I was fourteen or so, young in my faith, I had a vivid dream in which I was standing before Jesus. I saw this glorious light coming from a human form, but it was pure light. Every cell in my body wanted to fall down and worship Him, and that's exactly what I did because I immediately recognized that I was unworthy to be in His presence. All I could do was avert my gaze, prostrate myself before Him, and say, "Thank you, Lord, for loving me."

That dream has stayed with me for more than forty years, which is a testament to the power of One who was and is both God and man: Jesus Christ. My experience with the Lord is why I forward a YouTube link to a three-minute, eighteen-second video to everyone on my email list every Good Friday. The presentation, called "That's My King," features a wonderful discourse from a black preacher, Dr. S.M. Lockridge, that has received more than 7.5 million views.[1]

Perhaps you've watched it. The marvelous cadence of Dr. Lockridge's presentation is slow and soulful, irresistible and impressive,
powerful and potent. Anyone hearing his spellbinding sermon can't
help getting goosebumps as he reels off a litany of attributes describing
the most powerful man to walk the earth:

My Bible says He's the King of the Jews.

He's the King of Israel.

He's the King of righteousness.

He's the King of the ages.

He's the King of Heaven.

He's the King of glory.

He's the King of kings, and He is the Lord of lords.

That's my King.

I wonder: Do you know Him?

My King is a sovereign King.

No means of measure can define His limitless love.

He's enduringly strong.

He's entirely sincere.

He's eternally steadfast.

He's immortally graceful.

He's imperially powerful.

He's impartially merciful.

Do you know Him?

Because Jesus is imperially powerful, it's intimidating writing
about the power of one man when it comes to Jesus Christ, who was
both God and man, a difficult concept to wrap our heads around. So
bear with me as I give it a shot.

I begin with Luke 2:49 (NKJV) in which Jesus said, "Did you not
know that I must be about my Father's business?"

I take this to mean that the kingdom of God is a family business.
Let's ruminate on that a bit.

In other words, God the Father is the founder and chairman of the board. Jesus is the chief executive officer, and the Holy Spirit is the chief operating officer. The twelve apostles were the original board members, and we are the franchise owners.

Carrying this business metaphor a step further—if General Motors makes cars and McDonald's makes burgers and fries, what business is the kingdom of God in?

Jesus says we—the franchise owners—are to go and make disciples of all nations, baptizing them in the name of the Father and of the Son and of the Holy Spirit, and teaching them to obey everything Jesus has commanded them to do (Matthew 28:19–20a NIV).

So we're to make disciples...but what exactly are disciples?

In Christianity, disciples are generally described as dedicated followers of Jesus. This term is found only in the New Testament in the four gospels and the Book of Acts. Jesus emphasizes that being one of His disciples can be costly:

> A large crowd was following Jesus. He turned around and said to them, "If you want to be my disciple, you must, by comparison, hate everyone else—your father and mother, wife and children, brothers and sisters—yes, even your own life. Otherwise, you cannot be my disciple. And if you do not carry your own cross and follow me, you cannot be my disciple.
>
> "But don't begin until you count the cost. For who would begin construction of a building without first calculating the cost to see if there is enough money to finish it? Otherwise, you might complete only the foundation before running out of money, and then everyone would laugh at you. They would say, 'There's the person who started that building and couldn't afford to finish it!'

"Or what king would go to war against another king without first sitting down with his counselors to discuss whether his army of ten thousand could defeat the twenty thousand soldiers marching against him? And if he can't, he will send a delegation to discuss terms of peace while the enemy is still far away. So you cannot become my disciple without giving up everything you own."
—Luke 14:25–33 (NLT)

In making disciples, Jesus uses the raw material that comes to Him, just as McDonald's turns potatoes into French fries and GM takes an ingot of iron and makes an engine valve out of it. The raw material I'm referring to is us: sinful people. We are the lost persons who come to the factory, which is the church of Jesus Christ. It's the church that takes young Christians and turns them into apprentices and eventually into disciples who preach the Gospel with both word and deed, prepared to share the hope we have in Christ for eternal life. Disciples spread the Good News in love, mercy, and grace.

According to our CEO, the One who oversees all operations and ensures we produce the desired results consistent with His overall strategy and mission for our lives, the second thing disciples are supposed to do is restore sight to the blind.

That means each of us is to provide vision to others as a man of God, as a leader, as a father, and as a brother, to go boldly where no man has gone before. Proverbs 29:18a (KJV) says, "Where there is no vision, the people perish."

We do that by reminding people that the kingdom of God is a place of forgiveness, a place of possibility, a place of miracles, a place of love, a place of collaboration, a place of restoration, and a place of redemption. We are to bring Heaven down to this earth and give people a vision of what that looks like.

The third thing the mission requires is for us to heal the broken-hearted. Everyone agrees we are living in unique times with great political turmoil and unrest in city streets. People are depressed, suicidal, and feeling abandoned. It's our job to start the healing process by reminding the brokenhearted who they are in Christ. It's our job to say, "God is for you, so who can be against you?"

So many people need healing today—healing that comes from a foundation of love, mercy, and grace. We should be in the business of restoration, not condemnation.

Years ago in the mid-1990s, Dwight L. Carlson wrote an intriguing book titled *Why Do Christians Shoot Their Wounded?* Carlson demonstrated that many emotional problems are just as physical or biological as diabetes or heart disease. "So why do many Christians treat the emotionally ill as sinners instead of wounded saints who need a helping hand?" asked the author.

That's a great question. Our answer should come straight from Galatians 6:1 (NLT):

> Dear brothers and sisters, if another believer is overcome by some sin, you who are godly should gently and humbly help that person back onto the right path. And be careful not to fall into the same temptation yourself.

I love this Scripture because God uses greatly those who have been deeply wounded. I've seen this happen in others, and I've seen this happen in myself: the greater the wound, the greater the anointing.

The fourth thing we're called to do is to set free those who are in captivity—those in bondage to alcohol, to drugs, to sex, and a whole host of other addictions. There's a close correlation between the Beatitudes of Jesus found in Matthew 5:1–12 and the twelve-step program found in many recovery organizations. Abbie Earnest, director of the Christian 12 Step Ministry, outlines how the road to recovery is based on the Beatitudes:[2]

Step 1: I realize I'm not God; I admit that I am powerless to control my tendency to do the wrong thing, and that my life is unmanageable.

Happy are those who know they are spiritually poor.

Step 2: I earnestly believe that God exists, that I matter to Him, and that He has the power to help me recover.

Happy are those who mourn, for they shall be comforted.

Step 3: I consciously choose to commit all my life and will to Christ's care and control.

Happy are the meek.

Steps 4–5: I openly examine and confess my faults to myself, to God, and to someone I trust.

Happy are the pure in heart.

Steps 6–7: I voluntarily submit to any and all changes God wants to make in my life and humbly ask Him to remove my character defects.

Happy are those whose greatest desire is to do what God requires.

Steps 8–9: I evaluate all my relationships and offer forgiveness to those who have hurt me and make amends for harm I've done to others when possible, except when to do so would harm them or others.

Happy are the merciful.

Steps 10–11: I reserve a time with God for self-examination, Bible reading, and prayer in order to know Him and His will for my life and to gain the power to follow it.

Happy are the peacemakers.

Step 12: I yield myself to God to be used to bring this Good News to others, both by my example and my words.

Happy are those who are persecuted because they do what God requires.

◆   ◆   ◆   ◆

So what was Jesus's leadership style as one man?

As with most things, Jesus turned leadership upside down. He taught the disciples that in the Kingdom they were not to lead people as those in the world did; they were to be radically different. "So the last will be first, and the first last," He said (Matthew 20:16a NKJV).

The leadership style that Jesus modeled was not about command and control or status and power. He did not teach techniques or processes. Instead, He taught about growing character—a character centered on a Christlike servant's heart. He modeled servanthood and challenged His disciples to follow His example—to be like Him. From a Kingdom perspective, this makes a leadership style modeled on Jesus and centered on His indwelling characteristics superior to all secular leadership styles.

Consider these points:

- *It shall not be so among you...* For the most part, Christian colleges teach very little about how to lead people, creating a vacuum in which information on how to lead comes from outside the Kingdom. Business gurus with worldly outlooks have developed these styles with the aim of maximizing the benefit gained from "human resources," as if individuals can be looked upon as a commodity.

Jesus pointed the disciples to leaders in the world and told them, "It shall not be so among you" (Matthew 20:26a ESV).

- *The greatest among you...* The world's conception is that those who lead are in some ways better than the

people they lead. They gain status because they exercise
power over others to achieve their goals—all of which
leads to rewards, benefits, and preferential treatment,
and none of which impresses Jesus. He took the scribes
and Pharisees to task for such behavior (Matthew 23:1–
11), showing that behavior reflects the nature of the
heart (Luke 6:43–45).

Jesus's leadership style is diametrically opposed to that of the
world. He declared that greatness belongs to the servant with childlike
humility (Matthew 18:4). He taught that leaders were to serve others,
not to be served by them.

- *That you also should do just as I have done to
  you*...Jesus's heart was a servant's heart (Philippians
  2:5–11), from which His behavior flowed. This heart
  led Him to act for the benefit and growth of others. This
  He demonstrated to the disciples through the visual
  parable of foot-washing. He challenged them to follow
  His example (John 13:12–17), a challenge for leaders
  that echoes down through the centuries to us today.
- *The wisdom of this world is folly*...Jesus's leadership
  style reflects the way of the Kingdom of God (Matthew 18:4) and is the essence of the character of Christ
  (Matthew 20:28), which is why it's radically different
  than natural cultures in all countries and organizations. His leadership style is not the way of the world,
  whose wisdom is folly in the eyes of God (1 Corinthians 3:19). The way of Christ is one we should follow,
  however foreign it may seem to us from how we were
  raised or taught.

So what might such a Christ-centered, servant-hearted leadership look like? Briefly, I will summarize ten perspectives on leadership modeled on Jesus's leadership style.

1. Nurture a Christlike servant-hearted character. Jesus had a sacrificial servant's heart focused on the needs of others. Ask yourself: "How can I live out Christ's servant-hearted character, putting first concern for those whom I lead?"

2. Focus on others. Serve others so they can grow and be effective in God's service. Ask yourself: "What else can I do to enable each person I lead to achieve his or her full potential?"

3. Take responsibility for understanding. Effective communication is essential, so take responsibility. Ask yourself: "What can I do to ensure that others have understood me and that I have understood them?"

4. Consider the individual. Make cooperation more effective by developing the best relationships you can with those you lead. Ask yourself: "How can I improve the manner in which we work together by adjusting how I interact with each person?"

5. Nurture the character of Christ. Encourage others to live out Christlike values. Ask yourself: "How can I affirm those who are honest and truthful, and how can I better reflect Christ's love by treating everyone with honesty and dignity?"

6. Model the way. Like it or not, you are a role model to those whom you lead, and actions speak louder than words. Ask yourself: "How can I make my values to be more Christlike and live them out in front of those whom I lead?"

7. Inspire a shared vision. A shared vision of purpose and outcome, which is owned by all, is the key to achieving the goal. Ask yourself: "How can I engage my team to build a shared vision that encourages greater levels of cooperation?"

8. Challenge the process. It's always possible to be more effective, making it easier to achieve the desired outcomes. Ask yourself:

"How can I encourage my team to continually find better ways of doing things?"

9. Enable others to achieve. Our goal is to enable others to achieve. Ask yourself: "How can I better equip and empower those whom I lead to more easily reach and fulfill our shared vision?"

10. Encourage the heart. Knowing that one is valued is an important encouragement for everyone. Ask yourself: "How can I publicly and genuinely recognize the value of individuals and their achievements?"

You have just tasted some of what it means to grow a servant's heart as a leader and live out Jesus's leadership style.

As one man, Jesus as CEO changed the world. Today as His franchise owners, we're called to make disciples through coaching and conversation. When other men see and hear our transparency, it's amazing how real talk will draw men to share their stories and create a bond. And when you're transparent, you're practicing humility, which never goes out of style.

I know that in the times when I've been vulnerable and broken, I was amazed how many men came to me to share the same vulnerability and brokenness, which led to penetrating discussions in which I could tell them that Jesus is close to the brokenhearted and saves those who are crushed in spirit (Psalm 34:18). God is closer than you realize, and He can save you from despair.

◆   ◆   ◆   ◆

Now I want to talk about the power of one man as it relates to Jesus, a model for servant leadership. I begin with what I call the "principle of the twelve."

Have you ever thought about how many times the number twelve appears in human constructs? We have the number on the top of a clock. We have twelve months in a year.

In the Bible, we have the twelve tribes of Israel. We have twelve disciples. In the Book of Revelation, there are twelve gates in God's Kingdom and twelve angels guarding those gates. Twelve beautiful stones will be used to build the New Jerusalem's foundation. The number twelve is mentioned 187 times in Scripture and twenty-two times in Revelation. Twelve is considered to be a perfect number, symbolizing God's power and authority as well the completeness of the nation of Israel.

When it comes to leading people, Jesus spent more than three years teaching the twelve apostles, coaching them, building them up. Imagine being one of the disciples at the time. You saw Him raise the dead. You saw Him feed five thousand with what was basically a Happy Meal. You saw Him walk on water. You saw Him say to Mother Nature, "Be still and take a chill pill." You saw Him give sight to the blind and heal the woman who'd bled all her life. He cast out demons and sent a herd of pigs running down a hill and into a lake, where they drowned.

Yet after years of training, observing, and experiencing Jesus, one of His apostles betrayed Him, another doubted Him, and all but one deserted Him when He went to His death. Only John had the courage to stand with Him outside the city gate while He hung on a cross.

The lesson for us is that when you lead, when you become that one man, when you accept the call like Noah, Abraham, or David and say yes to God, then be prepared to be denied. Be prepared to be doubted. Be prepared to be betrayed. Be prepared to be deserted.

And yet Jesus, while hanging on the cross in the moment of His greatest agony, looked out and said, "Father, forgive them for they know not what they do." That is the key of the one-man concept that Jesus modeled for us.

I know many of you are carrying burdens. Some of you have never forgiven your father for deserting you. Some of you have never forgiven your mother for having an affair that tore up your family. Some of you had teachers who told you that you'd never make it in life. Some of you have been betrayed by youth leaders or by someone who took sexual advantage of you. Some of you just have been through hell and high water, and yet you're stuck in so much misery and pain that all you can do is just hold it in.

What Jesus is saying, as our one-man example, is this: "If you want to see like Me, if you want to overcome death and the grave, if you want to transcend the adversity of life, the first thing you've got to do is look out at those who have harmed you and say, 'I forgive you.'"

Forgiveness means you no longer hold people accountable for what they did to you. You don't brandish the receipt and keep reminding them of what they did. In order to become the one man that God wants to use to transform your family, your community, and your job, I urge you to take this important first step to forgive. You've got to let it go.

Understand that God knows the worst things about you. All the bad thoughts. All the mess-ups. All the mistakes. All the secrets that nobody knows about. All the ranting. All the anger. All the sins.

And yet, He still loves you. He says if you confess your sins, He will cleanse you of all unrighteousness. "I will throw your sins as far as the east is from the west," He says. "I will throw your sin in the sea of forgetfulness and remember it no more."

When you want to be a leader, to be that one man, Jesus is your model. Don't lose your mind when somebody betrays you. Don't give up because somebody denies you. Don't quit because somebody doubts you. That's what you must be prepared for.

It's interesting how the one person you can't stand turns out to be someone you see again and again and again. That person could be of a different race, the opposite gender, or a different age, but what God is saying is that until you forgive and live, you cannot become the one man He needs you to be. To become that one man, you must learn the lesson of forgiveness.

◆   ◆   ◆   ◆

One of the greatest examples of unconditional forgiveness comes in the story of the Prodigal Son, a parable in which Jesus gives us our one-man model.

When the Prodigal Son asked for his inheritance, what he was really saying to his father was this: "I want you to die. I'd rather have my money than you."

Does that sound familiar? Doesn't it sound like us when we pray? We don't want the Giver. We want the gift. We don't want the Promiser. We want the promise.

This young guy takes his stuff and goes off to party, a lifestyle that's unsustainable in the long run. Not too much time passes before he's broke, busted, and disgusted. Things get so bad that "he would gladly have filled his stomach with the pods that the swine ate, and no one gave him anything" (Luke 15:16 NKJV).

Note two things about this sentence of Scripture:

1. Pigs were anathema to Jewish people, dating back to the days of Deuteronomy when God forbade the Hebrews from eating or even touching them. They were "unclean" animals, so for the Prodigal Son to even step inside a pig pen was an awful thing to do.
2. The Bible doesn't say that the Prodigal Son ate the pig's food but that he "would gladly have" done so, which means that even the pigs wouldn't share their slop with him.

Now that's how low he had fallen. In his culture, he couldn't fall lower than that, but that's where the young man found himself. He had nothing. No home. No family. No friends. No food. No opportunity.

Some of you reading this book may find yourselves standing outside the pig pen. You're ready to hop the fence and grab that corn husk, that bruised apple, that rotten egg—and eat awful things that you never thought you'd consume.

Some of you are looking in the mirror after an all-night binge. Some of you are in a house with a woman who's not your wife, and you're looking at yourself, saying, "What's become of me?" Some of you are at the gambling table and have already lost enough money to pay the rent.

No matter where you are, God wants you to come home. No matter how badly you've messed that up, no matter how low you are, you can acknowledge where you are and realize your Father has a home for you.

But I can't go back, Ron.

That's what the Prodigal Son thought too.

I've ruined my father's name. I've destroyed his credit. His name is in the mud because I'm the reflection of my father, and I've messed it up. I can't go back.

That's what the devil wants you to believe. He wants you thinking that you've gone so far down, that you've sinned so badly, that there's no way you can ever go back.

The Prodigal Son thought about his plight and decided, *Well, maybe I can't go back as a son, but I can become his hired hand. I hope he'll have enough mercy on me to let me work with the horses and the cattle.*

As the Prodigal Son is walking down the road broken and humbled, the father who has been worried sick about him, the father who's been waiting up day and night to hear news of him, sees him in the distance.

Scripture tells us while the Prodigal Son was still a ways off, his father knew what he wanted to do. "Filled with love and compassion, he ran to his son, embraced him, and kissed him," says Luke 15:20b (NLT).

A couple of things are going on here. First, grown men did not run in those days. One, running was viewed as unseemly for an adult male in that culture, and two, how could you run while wearing a full-length tunic? So for the father to take off in a sprint meant that he had to grip the bottom of his tunic, pull it up, and bare his legs. You didn't do that back then because bare legs equaled humiliation.

And yet the father was willing to open himself up to disgrace.

But there's something else to consider: the father decided to run because he wanted to get to his son *before* he entered the village and heard snide remarks and experienced rejection.

The father modeled how Jesus will treat us when we repent, when we make a U-turn from sin, when we decide to follow Him and walk in His path.

The father wasn't full of religion; he was full of compassion. He wasn't full of tradition; he was full of compassion. What he executed at that moment was forgiveness. He restored his son and killed the fatted calf in celebration.

And the Prodigal Son became one man.

◆   ◆   ◆   ◆

Not everyone will celebrate your one-man calling. Not everyone will celebrate the gift that God has given you. Not everyone will be applauding when you accept the call to become the one man to change your marriage, change your family, change your church, or change the community. Some will deny you as the people in Nazareth denied Jesus.

Remember, there are three ways you can look at Jesus. He is either Lord, liar, or lunatic, as author and apologist C.S. Lewis said one time. The Pharisees thought he was a liar. Some of his own family thought he was crazy ("'He's out of his mind,' they said" [Mark 3:21b NLT]). But don't let that discourage you from seeing Him as Lord, even though much of the world doesn't see Him that way.

There are people who will see you the same way when you announce what God has given you to do as one man in His Kingdom. The new business you want to start, the new church plant you want to do, the new ministry you want to unleash, the new book you want to write, the new online website to bring families together you want to launch, or the new outreach to young people in the inner city—some will see you as a lunatic to even think you can make a difference. They will see you as a liar because you won't keep your word, or they'll see you as the Lord's man. You have to adopt His attributes of love, compassion, and kindness.

It's Jesus's attributes that compel me to send out Dr. Lockridge's emotional and excellent description of who Jesus is and the majesty and power of His Name every year at Easter. Many people think they know Jesus, but they don't.

I don't want Jesus to be a historical figure to you—like George Washington or Abraham Lincoln, someone you learned about in Sunday School or sitting in a church pew. I want you to have a deep understanding of the majesty, of the perfection, of the holiness, and of the righteousness of God's Son. Dr. Lockridge did a magnificent job of helping us understand the height, depth, breadth, length, and width of the deity, the divine nature, and the beauty of who Jesus is:

You can't get Him out of your mind.

You can't get Him off of your hands.

You can't outlive Him.

And you can't live without Him.

The Pharisees couldn't stand Him, but they found out they couldn't stop Him.

Pilate couldn't find any fault in Him.

The witnesses couldn't get their testimonies to agree.

Herod couldn't kill Him.

Death couldn't handle Him.

And the grave couldn't hold Him.

Yeah! That's my King!

That's why I'm asking you to take the time to watch and listen to this wonderful exposition about the fullness of God's glory. If and when you do watch, I wouldn't be surprised if you're moved to tears or on your feet clapping. You will be left with a feeling of awe and wonderment because Someone was willing to go the cross, take your sins on His shoulders, and die for you.

On that Good Friday, He decided to take the cup that He wanted God to remove from His hand, looked into the future toward you, and said, "I love you so much. I'm going to change destiny. I'm going to change a life. I'll be the one man who won't let you down. I'll be the one man who will not reject you. I'll be the one man who will love you. I'll be the one man who will restore you. I'll be the one man who will forgive you. I'll be the one man who will stand by you. I'll be the one man who will inspire you. I'll be the one man who'll motivate you.

"I will be the one man who, if you let Me, will change your life from bad to good. From rejection to selection. From brokenness to restoration. I am the one man who can change your pain into power and your scars into stars. I am the one man. I am the Alpha and the Omega. The first and the last. If you let Me, I'll make you the one man because I am the man."

◆　　　◆　　　◆　　　◆

I mentioned in Chapter 3 how I made a commitment to fast at the start of 2020. Now I'd like to share a bit more about how *the* one man, Jesus Christ, made me a better person and helped me overcome my addiction to carbohydrates.

All my life I've struggled with my weight. When I was a kid, I had too much chunk in the trunk, as they say. Mom would escort me to the "husky" section whenever I needed new clothes.

Following puberty, though, I shed much of my baby fat and became lean and mean. I was fit during high school, busy and active. Then came my early twenties when I got married, had a couple of kids, and worked two or three jobs. I didn't have time to work out but I sure found time to work my fork to my mouth. If I sat down on the couch to watch my beloved Cleveland Browns play on Sunday afternoons, I'd hold a big bag of Lay's potato chips on my lap. I couldn't eat just one chip, as the advertisements dared me to do. I had to consume the entire bag!

The same went for Doritos, Fritos, Cheetos…once I put that salty taste into my system, some kind of engine took over. The same feeling came over me whenever I sat down for a meal: I couldn't say no to the stack of pancakes, the heaping plate of fries, the fresh hamburgers coming off the grill, or the delicious fixings for tacos. I was an equal-opportunity eater. I had to have those carbs.

Naturally, I put on weight over the years. A ton of weight. Too much weight. So as the New Year approached in 2020, I cried out to the Lord, "Help me!"

This was the same cry I uttered when I was sexually abused as a young boy, the same cry I made when I would bang my head against the wall at night because the kids at school made fun of my stuttering. I distinctly remember lying down on the floor and praying, "God, please help me so I can have more energy so I can be a better man, a better husband, a better father, and a better leader."

And so I began my annual fast to start the New Year, just as I described earlier. It was my wife, Rachel, who suggested this to me: "Why don't you focus on abiding in Christ? Take this time to be still."

Abiding isn't a word you hear much these days, but it's certainly used in Scripture, especially by the Apostle John when he quoted Jesus as saying:

> If you abide in me, and my words abide in you, ask what-
> ever you wish, and it will be done for you.
> —John 15:7 (ESV)

I looked up the Greek word for *abide* and found that it means "to stay, to live with, to walk with in an intimate way." It's like a mother kangaroo traveling everywhere with a baby kangaroo in her pouch; they abide together.

So as I chose to do my best to "abide" in the Lord during my fast, my great prayer was that He would take away my addiction to carbohydrates. I leaned on this passage:

> Take my yoke upon you. Let me teach you, because I am humble and gentle at heart, and you will find rest for your souls. For my yoke is easy to bear, and the burden I give you is light.
> —Matthew 11:29–30 (NLT)

After seven days of truly abiding with Him, this became the easiest fast I'd ever done. My cravings were swept away. My desires for junk food disappeared. I felt renewed, so much so that I was able to maintain my fast for fifty days and lose—lose!—sixty pounds. This was something I never could have done on my own strength.

Things that seem impossible with man are possible with one man, Jesus Christ. He's ready for you to take a step toward Him so that He can make you a new man.

Become that new man today.

◆   ◆   ◆   ◆

Discussion Questions

1. Who is Jesus to you? Is He Lord, liar, or lunatic?
2. Have you accepted Jesus Christ as your personal savior? Talk about why or why not.

3. Do you share your faith in Christ on a regular basis with those around you?
4. How do you feel that Jesus has made you a new man?
5. What's the best thing Jesus has done for you and your life?

10

One Man's Story: A Personal Story

After graduating from Baldwin Wallace University in the mid-1980s, I got a big break when I was hired by the Eaton Corporation in downtown Cleveland, where I was able to put my energy and growing skills in organizational management to good use. Working alongside Eaton's experts in Open Space Technology (OST)—a new approach to holding meetings, conferences, and corporate retreats in a way that facilitated purpose-driven leadership—was a tremendous experience. Eaton was a fantastic firm to work for, and being paid a handsome salary allowed me to access the American Dream. From a material side, things couldn't have been better.

From a spiritual standpoint, things were cooking too. I hadn't been settled in my downtown office very long when the elders at First Baptist Church in Berea—where St. Peter Chanel was located—inquired about me becoming their pastor. It seemed that their ninety-year-old pastor was hoping to retire and rest his feet a bit before the Lord Jesus welcomed him to Heaven.

One morning, one of the church elders called and explained the situation. "Can you come in and help us?" he inquired.

"But I have a full-time job," I said, taking time to explain my corporate position with Eaton.

"That's fine. You just show up to preach on Sunday and we'll take care of the rest," the elder said. "We can offer you $250 a week."

Because of the pastor's advanced age, the congregation had dwindled down to fifty hardy souls. Since I could continue my climb up the corporate ladder—remember, I was twenty-three years old and wanted to make my mark just like anyone else coming out of college—I said yes. I thought this was the best of both worlds.

Under my preaching, the church grew. Actually, First Baptist did more than grow—it exploded. We went from the core membership of fifty men, women, and children to around five hundred people in the first year. I loved preaching His Word and pointing out a path to eternal salvation through our Lord Jesus Christ.

I also received much joy from seeing new people join us on Sunday mornings, perhaps darkening a church door for the first time in ages. One of those new persons was someone very special to me: my grandmother, Greta. I loved having Grannie sitting in the front.

For a white woman in a black church, Grannie fit in well, but then again, she had been living in the "black world" for many years. She also adapted quickly to the black church tradition, where it's OK to "interact" with the preacher, as in shouting out, "Amen, pastor!" or "Preach it, brother!" during the sermon. As I would soon learn, Grannie wasn't afraid to throw in her two cents. She could be loud.

Now, I like to preach "thorough" sermons, which means I can be a little long. The average sermon is thirty minutes. Well, one Sunday morning, I had been going on for an hour, and I still had a ways to go.

"Now let me talk a bit about point six," I said.

Grannie exhaled a long sigh that could be heard all the way to the back of the church. "This is ridiculous," she said out loud. "People have to pee!"

The entire church cracked up. She had no filter.

First Baptist Church happened to be located next door to the Cleveland Browns' training facility. In fact, the church backed up to the main football field.

Because of the proximity, the Browns heard some good things about me, so I was invited to become one of the team chaplains. Being part of the NFL was a great experience and gave me a chance to minister to and mentor young men—many of whom were black athletes from humble surroundings, just like I had come from growing up.

Chapel was held on Saturday nights in the team hotel since the players had to be sequestered under the same roof on the eve of every game, home and away. Attendance was voluntary—but of those who came, I had their attention, man. They were not playing a game; football was life and death for them. They wanted to hear something about God and about eternal life with Him as they went into battle for themselves and their family members.

In meeting individually with these NFL players, many of them told me how they had grown up without a father in the home. The issue of fatherlessness, which I discussed in Chapter 2, was something I could personally relate to.

Sometimes our discussions reminded me that there was still a small hole in my heart. Or maybe it was a longing...a longing to know who my real father was. Where did I come from? Who was my dad? Those were unanswered questions that I could never put out of my mind, and I knew they might never be answered.

Every now and then, though, I couldn't help but think there was someone out there who was my father. Most likely he had no idea as well, given Mom's profession at the time. When these feelings came to the surface, I had to stuff them back down. That's how I got through...it's what I had done ever since adolescence.

When I was twenty-eight years old, my mom's brother, Uncle Buster, moved to Austin, Texas, to work a big construction job. One day, he happened to go to the county courthouse for some reason. Inside the main corridor, he noticed a well-dressed black man carrying a leather briefcase walking toward him. He was in his mid-forties with short-cropped hair and was wearing a suit and tie. He looked like an attorney on his way to a court hearing.

Buster met his eyes—and received the shock of his life. He stopped the man in his tracks and said, "Oh my gosh—I know you."

The well-dressed man halted his progress. "Excuse me?"

"Are you from Cleveland?"

A surprised look came across the attorney's face. "Well, yes..."

That was all the confirmation Uncle Buster needed. "I remember you from the old neighborhood. You're Ron Sullivan!"

The attorney's face lit up in recognition. "Wait a minute. You're Buster, Liz's brother!"

And then Uncle Buster said something that rocked Ron Sullivan's world: "You look just like my nephew. You have a son, man."

Ron clutched his chest. "What?" he stammered.

"Yeah, you and Liz had a baby!"

Now Ron was staggering. "Really?"

"I'm telling ya, you're the spittin' image of him."

Ron struggled for words. "What's his name?"

"He was named Ronaldo in honor of our Cuban heritage, but everyone calls him Ron. Ron Archer."

"Archer? You mean Liz got married?"

"Well, yes and no. But your son is doing great. He's twenty-eight now and has a great career going. He's a pastor on weekends and is quite the preacher."

"Wow." Ron Sullivan was too stunned to say more.

They exchanged phone numbers, and Ron left, shaking his head. He was married but had no children. He had a successful law practice. He was well-established in the community. And now this. To find out after all these years that he was a father short-circuited the synapses in his brain.

I have a son? Apparently so.

When Mom was a "working girl," she had boyfriends on the side. Ron Sullivan was one of them. When she became pregnant at the age of seventeen, she didn't know who the daddy was. She couldn't have known; she had too many sexual partners. Besides, she and Ron weren't together that long, and then he graduated from high school and was off to college. She'd lost track of him, so he was out of the picture.

After running into Uncle Buster, Ron felt guilty. He thought about a poor kid who'd grown up without a father, without his input, without his support, and without his love. Complicating matters was that he would have to tell his wife what happened years before they met.

It took him several months to deal with his conflicted feelings, and then he called my mom. She had already heard the news from Buster, so the shock and awe had worn off a bit. Still, their initial phone conversation was an extraordinary moment filled with emotion for the two of them.

Following the phone call, they exchanged photos. Ron's snapshots confirmed in Mom's mind as well as my aunts' and uncles' that he was indeed my father. In a subsequent phone call, she told him, "Yeah, I have to admit the truth. You two are twins."

At the same time, though, Mom was reluctant to tell me that my real father had contacted her. That was a protective measure on her part.

Six months after Ron bumped into Uncle Buster in Texas, he decided to head back to Cleveland. He applied for and got a job as a county prosecutor for Cuyahoga County.

Ron and Mom continued to talk after he and his wife moved to Cleveland. Finally, Mom felt it was time for me to know what had been happening. She called me at home one evening and said, "I know who your real father is, and he wants to meet you."

"What?"

That was the most stunning news I'd ever heard in my life. It was like time stood still. I have a father, and he wants to meet me.

I had a ton of questions, and she told me the whole story. When I got off the phone with Mom, I got on my knees and prayed. "God, You have answered every prayer that I have ever had," I began. "You have been so good to me. Are You really going to let me meet my dad? After all these years? Lord, You don't withhold any good thing from me. You are beyond goodness. What You've done is beyond words."

Mom told me to go to a certain courtroom in the Cuyahoga County courthouse at a certain time, when my father would be prosecuting a case. When there was a break in the proceedings, he'd walk out of the courtroom to meet me.

I was nervous and excited at the same time. But what if doesn't like me? What if he rejects me? I had the same worries that Mom had.

At the correct time, I walked up to the courtroom, which had windows on each side of the entrance door. I peeked inside—and saw him returning to the prosecutor's table after approaching the bench. Right away, I noticed that he had the same complexion, the same hairline, the same moustache, and the same gait. He definitely looked like me.

I watched in amazement as he took a seat and resumed the hearing. He had all my mannerisms, including the way he held his head. *Oh, my God!*

I waited nervously until the court session went into recess. Through the window, I watched my father gather papers into a briefcase and walk toward the back door. I stepped away.

When he came through the doors, I was waiting for him. He smiled. "Hello, Ron. I believe I'm your father. How are you?"

No better words had been said to me, but I couldn't answer—tears were running down my cheeks. My father started crying as well. We fell into each other's arms and sobbed.

"I'm so sorry it took so long. If I had known, I would have been around. But I didn't know. I'm truly sorry."

I wiped away several tears. "You don't have to apologize. It's OK. It's really OK."

"This is so overwhelming."

"I wholeheartedly agree."

We continued chatting for a few minutes, and then he had to return to the courtroom. "Can you come by tomorrow to my office, say around 10:00 a.m.?"

"Of course."

When I arrived the next day, my father introduced me to his colleagues. Then he said, "There's someone special you have to meet—Judge Franklin. He's been a mentor to me."

When we walked into the judge's chambers, an elderly black judge stood up from behind his desk.

"Judge Franklin, I have a surprise for you," my father said. "I have a son."

The old codger grunted. "You couldn't make a son if you had paper and a pencil," he said. And then the judge's eyes got big. "I take it back. I can clearly see the resemblance."

Eventually, my father took a paternity test to confirm that he was my birth father. We went out to dinner and saw movies together. We walked around the Cleveland Metroparks Zoo and the lakefront. We bonded like a father and son.

One time, he asked me if I could set aside a Saturday to meet his immediate family. Of course, I said yes.

Our first stop was his brother's house, where Uncle Leroy welcomed us to a dining room table filled with finger foods. Other family members streamed through the front door, and I met more cousins and relatives than I ever knew I had.

On another Saturday afternoon, my father asked me to take a drive with him. He picked me up at my apartment and drove me to the Lee-Harvard neighborhood that we both had grown up in.

Dad—I actually called him "Pops"—was in a reminiscing mood. "I know what your mom was involved in and how rough life was for her," he said. "We were so young. We didn't know any better."

I continued to listen as we drove past familiar streets. We were several miles from our old house on Stockbridge Avenue—where Mom was still living—when he came upon a small church on a street corner. He parked the car in the parking lot that adjoined the church, which was a bit weather-beaten and showing its age.

"You see this church?" he asked.

"Of course."

"Do you know who built it?"

"Of course not." I had no clue.

"Your grandfather built this church. You see, my father was a pastor. I was a rebellious PK, the pastor's kid who partied and drank and was wild. When I hit my teen years, I did not want to go to church. After I left home to go to college, I stopped going to church and have never gone back. I don't believe in God anymore. I'm more a Buddhist than anything."

I couldn't believe how my father was opening up to me. I felt like this was a huge breakthrough for him, especially because he knew I was a pastor. I didn't say anything, however. The last thing I was going to do was judge him or tell him he needed to get off the path he'd been following for many years.

"Let me tell you something about my father," he continued. "I'd find him in his study on his knees, praying out loud for God to protect and

Are You a Man Worth Following?

The power of one man can happen to you. To help you unlock that power, here is a series of questions to point you in the right direction:

- **Your mission.** Why did God call you? What is your purpose for living and being? Recall a time when you felt most alive, most useful, most fulfilled. What were you doing and where were you?
- **Your message.** What do you have to overcome that God can use to inspire and help others?
- **Your method.** What biblical principles will you use to build toward your mission? Think about forgiveness, reconciliation, discipline, fasting, improved communication, humility, and consistency.
- **Your ministry.** What will be your God-centered strategy to accomplish God's mission? Is it to start a men's fellowship? Is it to begin a mentoring program? Is it to host marriage retreats? Is it to coach a youth sports league?
- **Your weaknesses.** What are the areas you need to be held accountable for with other men? In what areas do you need coaching and mentoring? What is your plan to become the one man who can change your family and community?
- **Your strengths.** List five things—things you do very well—that you are most proud of as a man. What can you teach other men about the strengths you've acquired?
- **Your future.** The power of one man starts with you—today!

lead to Himself the generations not yet born. He prayed for you before you were born, and he prayed for you not knowing that you were alive."

I was deeply moved and realized that God had chosen to honor the prayer of an old pastor—a grandfather I never knew.

For the next five years, Pops and I made up for lost time. We continued to do everything fathers and sons do—going to ballgames and the movies, as well as eating out together. My father and I developed a close relationship.

One evening, he called me on the phone. "Son, I'm losing my balance. I can't walk."

"I was just with you last weekend. What's wrong, Pops?"

He said he didn't know, but he was going to see a doctor in the morning. I immediately jumped in the car and drove over to his house. He looked terrible.

Blood work was done. Tests were run. And then his doctor sat him down to deliver difficult news: my father had cancer of the brain, cancer of the spinal cord, and cancer in his lymph nodes. Basically, he had cancer everywhere and was likely terminal. He was advised to put his "affairs in order."

The cause of his cancer, the doctor said, likely stemmed from a lifelong addiction to alcohol. Ever since he was a teenager, my father drank hard liquor—mainly vodka. He told the doctor that sometimes he would drink so much that alcohol would seep out his pores. He was still fighting his addiction demons when he met me.

Pops didn't give up hope. He submitted to chemotherapy, which is sometimes worse than the disease. His strength ebbed and his hair disappeared. He looked gaunt from the loss of weight.

I visited him on weekends, checking up on him. His body was wearing away. What was wearing on me, besides the toll that cancer was taking on him, was his spiritual health. In many ways, he was still the rebellious PK, shaking his fist at God.

One Saturday afternoon, I was sitting on the side of his bed. We were having a tender moment, and I felt the time was right to share Christ with him. But I knew I had to do it in a way that he would listen to since I didn't know if I would get another shot. I decided to start by asking him a question.

"Can I tell you a story?" I asked.

Pops looked at me. I saw trust in eyes that weren't as bright as they should be. He nodded his head perceptibly, so I proceeded.

Here's what I said:

"Once upon a time, there was a very powerful king who ruled over a vast empire. The pressure of the job was overwhelming at times, so as an outlet for his stress, the king brought in a court jester who would make him laugh and take his mind off of his troubles in far-flung reaches of his empire. The court jester entertained the king by juggling balls as he rode a unicycle, performing magic tricks, executing acrobatic tricks, and telling funny jokes. Because of his skill in making the king laugh, the monarch adored his court jester.

"One day, he called his court jester into his chambers and said, 'Because you are such a fool, I have an assignment for you.'

"The court jester didn't blink at being called a fool. His job, after all, was to be a fool. Then the king made known his request. 'I want you to go throughout my kingdom and search high and low, near and far, until you find a bigger fool than yourself. When you find that person, I want you to give him this golden rod.'

"The court jester said, 'Yes, sire!' At the same time, even though he was a fool, he thought the king's request was strange, but he knew he had no choice but to obey and go searching for a bigger fool than himself. The court jester traveled to farmlands, visited the cities, and points in between, each time stopping to interview people. He asked them questions and listened to their responses, but throughout his journey, he didn't find a bigger fool than himself.

"While out in the countryside, the court jester received a message that the king was gravely ill and would probably die soon. The message said, 'The king is devastated by the news. Please come back to see him before he dies.'

"The court jester was shocked as well. He raced back to the palace, where he found the king deathly ill and lying in bed.

"When the court jester walked into the monarch's chambers, the king said, 'My dear friend. It's so good to see your smiling face. Thank you for all the years of making me laugh, but the reality is that I'm going on a long, long journey from which I will never return.'

"The court jester looked at him with tears in his eyes, and he hugged the king gently. Both knew that the king was talking about his impending death.

"The court jester said, 'Sire, have you prepared for this long, long journey from which you will never return?'

"The king was befuddled and looked at him. 'Ah, no, I have not.'

"The court jester pulled the golden rod out of his satchel and gave it to the king. He had finally found someone who was a bigger fool than himself.

"He said to the king, 'The only thing that's guaranteed in this life is not wealth, not power, not success, and not even happiness. The only thing that's guaranteed is the end of it. Sire, you have written many policies. One is that people are to have home insurance in case their house burns down. That way, they can build a new home they can live in. You require that people have car insurance, in case their car gets damaged in a collision. You require that people have health insurance, in case they get sick. You require that everyone have life insurance, which is for those we leave behind.

"'But there is something you have not ordered or sought for yourself, and it's called death insurance. This type of insurance is not for your loved ones and not for your friends—it's for you. I'm talking about a policy called Jesus Christ Mutual Life. The beautiful news about it is that all the premiums have been paid for. All you have to do is ask to receive this death insurance.

"'And how do you receive it? If you confess with your mouth the Lord Jesus and believe in your heart that God raised Him from the dead, then you shall be saved.'"

My father was listening, but I could tell that I still hadn't gotten through. Remember, his heart had hardened over the years after walking away from God. So I tried a different tack.

"Let's forget everything else I just said about theology," I began. "You know a lot about business, so let me put things in a business perspective."

I knew my father was a frugal person who saved his money. He understood investments. He knew about risk management.

"The job of any businessman is to manage risk. Am I correct on that?"

"Yes."

"So if something happens, you want to be covered, right?"

"Right."

"The one thing you know for sure that will happen is death. So like the story says, do you have death insurance?"

Now I had his attention. I felt it was time to present the choice he needed to make.

"Let's say there's a fifty-fifty chance that everything I believe and your dad believed about Jesus is totally wrong. In other words, there is no God, there is no Heaven, and there is no Hell. You live your life, and then you die. You go to the grave, you're in the ground, and that's it. I'll give you that. On pure, statistical analysis, there's a 50 percent chance that could happen. But there's also a 50 percent chance I'm right—that if you die without Jesus Christ, you will spend eternity burning forever in a place called Hell. There's a 50 percent chance that

that risk exists, using pure, statistical analysis. So lying here in this bed, you're telling me that you're prepared to take that risk when you leave this earth? Is that good business?"

A serious look fell over my father's face. He was thinking. Then he had his answer.

"Hell, no, that's not good business. Oh, my God, I am the king in your story—the king who was a fool! You're right. Purely on statistics, you could be right, and I'm not prepared for the long journey awaiting me. At all! What must I do, son?"

We went through the Roman Road to salvation: that all have sinned and fallen short of the glory of God, that there is none righteous— no, not one. I explained how and why the wages of sin is death but the gift of God is eternal life through Christ Jesus. I took my time, and my father was intent on hearing every word.

"You know you are a sinner and cannot be right in your own strength," I said. "You know you have a sinful condition, and that makes you fall short. You know your body is going to die and doesn't live forever, but if you confess with your mouth the Lord Jesus and believe in your heart that God has raised Him from the dead, you shall be saved."

I said there's a three-step program that Jesus gave in His first public speech—the Sermon on the Mount.

"What's that?" my father asked.

"In Matthew 5, Jesus said, 'Blessed are the poor in spirit, for theirs is the kingdom of God.' This means you recognize your spiritual bankruptcy. You realize that you cannot get to God with your own currency because it's worthless. If you understand that, then you're on your way to the Kingdom of God.

"Two, Jesus said, 'Blessed are they that mourn, for they shall find succor.' When you recognize your sinful condition, then you are sorry for it and you repent of it. Now you have the ability to become a child of God and to inherit His Kingdom.

"Finally, Jesus said, 'Blessed are the meek, for they shall inherit the earth.' That's humility. You know you can't get there on your own. Blessed are those who hunger and thirst after righteousness, for they shall be filled. If you hunger after God, and you want His presence in your life, and you want salvation, He promises to fill you. That's where you are right now. Are you hungry and thirsty for God? Do you want to die without the blessed assurance, which is your insurance? Do you want to believe in Jesus and know you will spend eternity with Him?"

My father shifted in his bed. "Five years ago, God allowed me to meet you. He allowed me to be a father for the first time in my life and share my life with you. And here we are today. You are like my father, a man of God, and yet you never judged me, you never put me down, and you never got angry with me for not being in your life. You never once told me that I was unworthy or said, 'Where were you?' Instead, you showed me love and acceptance. You immediately became my son and let me be your father. You simply opened your heart and received me as your dad. The fact that you are telling me about these things before I die makes it clear to me that God sent you to me. Help me to pray, because I need to pray. I know there is a God, son."

We held hands, and then I asked him to close his eyes. I led my father through the Sinner's Prayer, and he accepted Jesus Christ as his personal Savior.

Amazing.

Absolutely amazing.

I had led many people—probably thousands—to the Lord since I started preaching at the age of sixteen. The opportunity to explain the Gospel to my father was an incredible experience. When I asked him to bow his head and pray to receive Christ into his heart, I wondered if I would be able to choke out the words. I somehow managed it in the sea of emotions that swelled in my innermost being.

For the next half-dozen months, Dad fought cancer. He had his good days and bad, but toward the end, he slipped into a coma and was in and out of consciousness. I was at his side when he died. As he neared the end, there was a death rattle. His breathing sped up. He took one last big breath, and then it was over.

Pops died when I was thirty-three years old. A memorial service was held at the House of Wills funeral home, but I couldn't officiate. I really couldn't. I just wanted to sit and take it all in.

I thought about how I had always wanted to know who my dad was. I thought about how God answered that prayer—as well as the prayer of a faithful pastor praying for unborn generations to come. I thought about the brief window we had together—five wonderful years. And I thought about how God used me—someone who really never should have been born—to bring my father to a saving knowledge of Jesus Christ.

That's when I understood the power of one man.

A BENEDICTION

As we come to a close, I'd like deliver my shortest sermon on record: *When God calls you to do something, He gives you a mission. He defines why you are alive and where you are going. Remember: God gave Noah a mission to build the ark. God gave Abraham the mission of starting the nation of Israel. God gave a teenage David the mission of becoming the next king. God gave Paul the mission of sharing the Gospel with the Gentiles.*

Your mission is always bigger than your ability, your talent, your pocketbook, your bank account, and your skill set. If you're waiting for the circumstances to be right, you will never fulfill your destiny in Christ. If you're waiting for everything you need to be perfectly in place, you'll never experience what God has in store for you.

What I've learned is that God wants you to give your natural 100 percent, and when you do that, you will experience the power of one man. The job of picking up and leaving behind everything he knew was bigger than Abraham. Goliath was bigger than David. The five thousand hungry people were bigger than the little boy's basket of fishes and loaves.

In other words, you will have to be prepared to struggle. You have to be prepared to climb. You will have to fight.

It's my closing prayer that the Lord will be with you every step of the way and help you experience the power of one man.

Because you can do it!

NOTES

Chapter 2: MIAs and POWs

1. "The Proof Is in: Father Absence Harms Children," National Fatherhood Initiative, https://www.fatherhood.org/fatherhood-data-statistics.
2. "The Consequences of Fatherlessness" fathers.com, http://fathers.com/statistics-and-research/the-consequences-of-fatherlessness/.
3. Wayne Parker, "Statistics on Fatherless Children in America," liveabout.com, May 24, 2019, https://www.liveabout.com/fatherless-children-in-america-statistics-1270392.
4. Jason DeParle and Sabrina Tavernise, "For Women under 30, Most Births Occur outside Marriage," *New York Times*, February 12, 2012, https://www.nytimes.com/2012/02/18/us/for-women-under-30-most-births-occur-outside-marriage.html.
5. Michael Maciag, "The Suicide Crisis," Governing, January 2015, https://www.governing.com/topics/health-human-services/gov-suicide-deaths-spike-in-rural-western-states.html.
6. Holly Hedegaard, Arialdi M. Miniño, and Margaret Warner, "Drug Overdose Deaths in the United States, 1999–2018," NCHS Data Brief, no. 356 (January 2020): https://www.cdc.gov/nchs/products/databriefs/db356.htm.

Chapter 3: A Strategy to Restore Men

1. Polly House, "Want Your Church to Grow? Then Bring in the Men," Baptist Press, April 3, 2003, http://www.bpnews.net/15630/want-your-church-to-grow-then-bring-in-the-men.

Chapter 4: One Man's Story: Noah and His Ark

1. Remember, I didn't know who my father was growing up, so I didn't have any relatives on my father's side.

Chapter 5: One Man's Story: Abraham, from Pimp to Prophet

1. Similar to how God changed Abram's name to Abraham, Sarai became Sarah.
2. It's believed that Abraham and his entourage entered Canaan in 2091 BC.

Chapter 7: One Man's Story: The Apostle Paul and His Road to Transformation

1. Some biblical scholars believe that Paul was also the author of the Book of Hebrews.

Chapter 8: The Power of Transformation

1. If you have any questions about undertaking this type of transformation, please contact me via the Places of Hope ministry at ron@placesofhope.com.

Chapter 9: One Man's Story: Jesus Christ, the Son of God

1. The pastor's initials stand for Shadrach Meshach, the names of two of the three figures from the third chapter of the Book of Daniel (the other was Abednego). They were three young Hebrew men who were thrown into a fiery furnace by Nebuchadnezzar, king of Babylon, when they refused to bow down to the king's image. The three suffered no harm, and the king witnessed four men walking in the flames—the fourth surely being the Son of God. "That's My King" was originally preached in 1976 in Detroit and is easily found on

YouTube. From 1952 until his retirement in 1993, Dr. Lockridge was pastor of Calvary Baptist Church in San Diego. He graduated to glory in 2000.

2. Abbie Earnest, "The Road to Recovery Based on the Beatitudes," October 28, 2013, https://www.christian12step.org/the-beatitudes-from-the-sermon-on-the-mount-and-the-12-steps-originated-from-alcoholics-anonymous/.

ABOUT THE AUTHORS

Ron Archer is an author, business executive, NFL chaplain, and leadership trainer for corporations and the military. Born prematurely to a seventeen-year-old single mother in the ghetto of Cleveland, Ohio, Archer had a severe learning disability and stuttering disorder when he was young. He experienced a radical spiritual transformation, which helped him discover his voice.

In 1984, Archer was awarded the Martin Luther King Jr. Leadership Award from Alpha Phi Alpha fraternity (Dr. King's fraternity) for becoming the second black Student Body President at Baldwin Wallace University, leading leadership classes, being president of the local Fellowship of Christian Athletes (FCA) and lead counselor for the local Upward Bound program, and leading revivals and Bible studies for the students and the community on the college campus.

Since then, he has traveled the globe, inspiring millions with his story. In 2014, a video of his life story went viral and has been watched by more than nine million people. He has traveled extensively throughout America and Central America and neighboring islands, reaching hundreds of thousands of people each year through his speaking engagements.

His website is ronarcher.org.

Mike Yorkey is the author, co-author, or collaborator of more than one hundred books, including the 2020 release of *What Belief Can Do* with Ron Archer. He is the co-author of *The Shot Caller* with Casey Diaz and the bestselling *Every Man's Battle* series, which has more than three million copies in print.

He and his wife, Nicole, reside in California. His website is mikeyorkey.com.